A Brief History of Black British Art

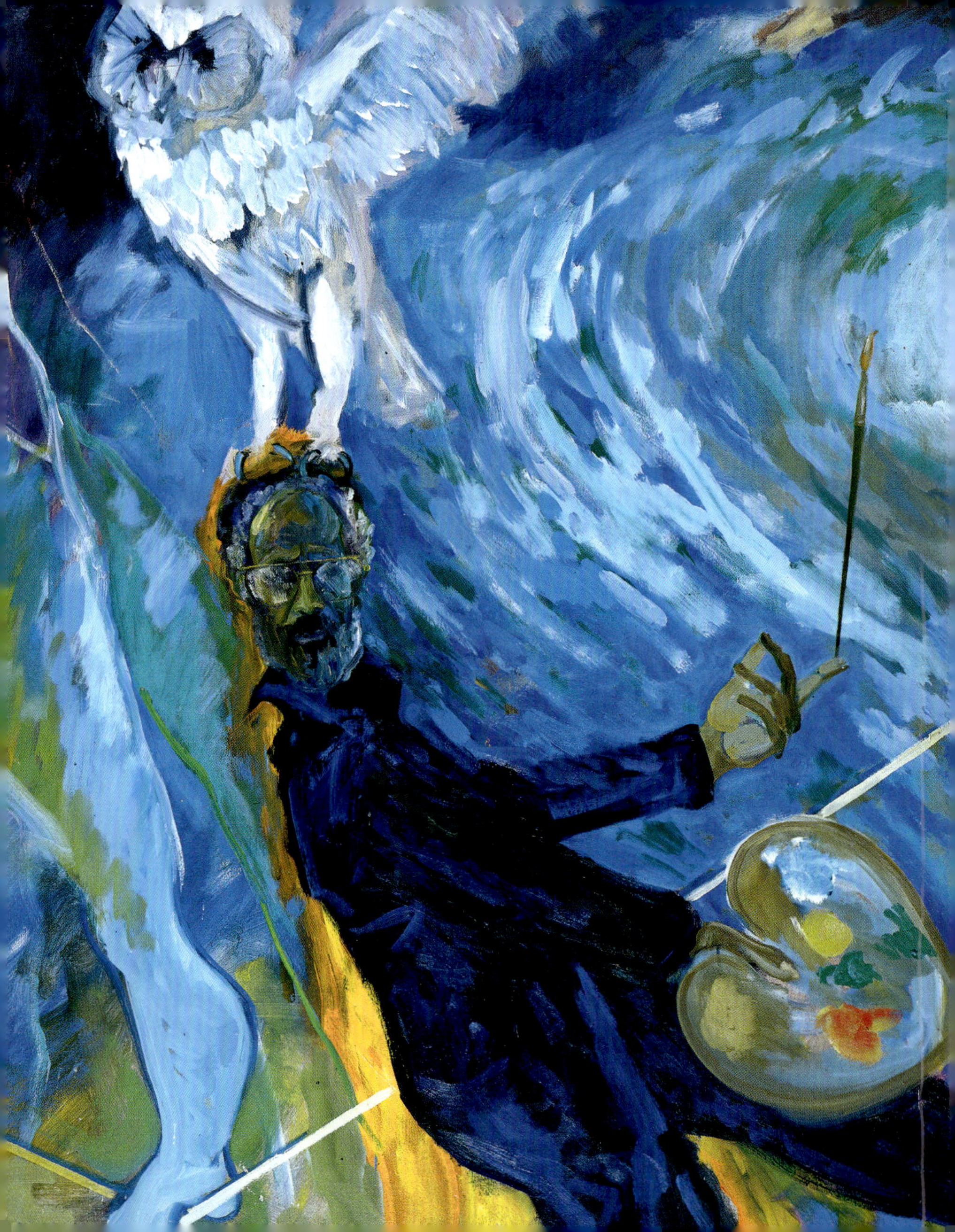

A Brief History of Black British Art

Rianna Jade Parker

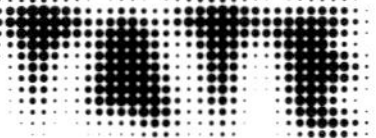

Thank you to Emma Poutler, Aurella Yussuf, Tracy Bohan,
and the Society of Authors for your diligence and kindness.

First published 2021 by order of the Tate Trustees
by Tate Publishing, a division of Tate Enterprises Ltd,
Millbank, London SW1P 4RG
www.tate.org.uk/publishing

A catalogue record for this book is available from the British Library
ISBN 978 1 84976 756 9

Distributed in the United States and Canada by ABRAMS, New York

Library of Congress Control Number applied for

Senior Editor: Emma Poulter
Production: Roanne Marner
Picture Researcher: Deborah Metherell
Designed by Hélène Baum-Owoyele
Colour reprographics by Altaimage, London
Printed and bound in Italy by Printer Trento S.r.l.

Front cover: Errol Lloyd *The Lesson* 1972 (see pp.44–5)
Back cover: Dennis Morris *Soul Sister, Hackney* 1974 (see pp.52–3)
Frontispiece: John Lyons *Self Portrait with Jumbie Bird and Alter Ego*
1990 (see pp.94–5)

Measurements of artworks are given in centimetres, height before
width and depth

Contents

'The Black soul, if there is such a thing, belongs in modernism.'

— **Frank Bowling**

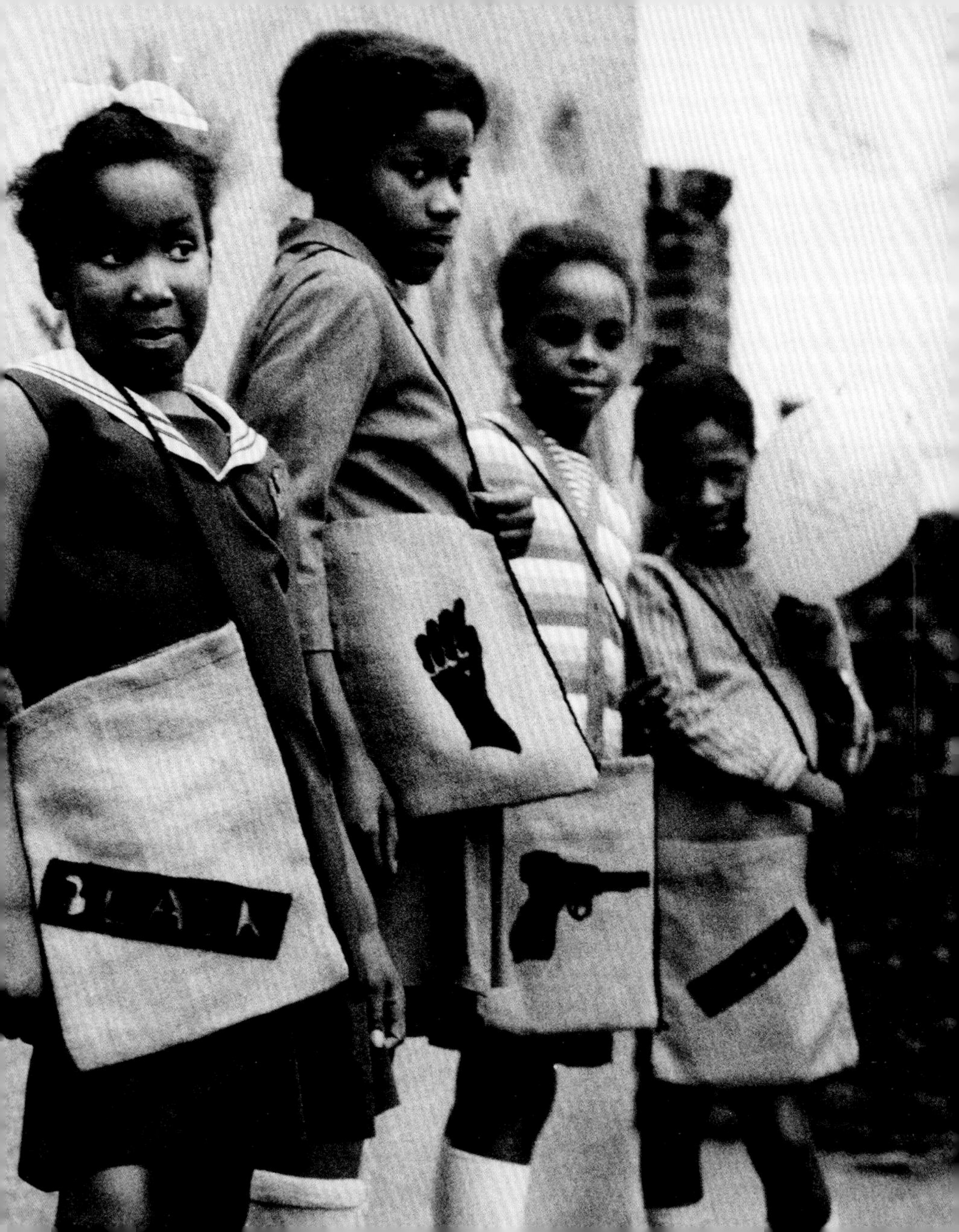

Defining Black British Art

Neil Kenlock b.1950
Black Panther School Bags
1970, printed 2010
Gelatin silver print on
paper 38.4 × 25. 3

When questioned about Black British Art in 1988, curator and historian Eddie Chambers revealed: 'The function of Black art, as I saw it a few years ago, was to confront the white establishment for its racism, as much as to address the Black community in its struggle for human equality. I think Black art still has that role to play.'[1] At the time of going to press with this book, over thirty years later, I would assert that work by Black artists still has this function, and to some extent the responsibility to assist in this struggle. Accepting the categorisation or not, first, second or third generations of Afro-descended immigrants have used their art-making not only to independently forge and fully acknowledge their identities, but as an outlet to challenge the rules of daily life while navigating the incomplete and often subordinate experience of 'Britishness' and citizenship which has always been unstable and temporal for Black people.

British-born West Indians and younger migrants who were educated and raised in the UK, were 'British' in many regards, but this was not reflected in their daily lives or living conditions, the discrimination they faced and their lack of social mobility. The alienation they experienced and the uncertainty of their place in society spearheaded the construction of Black Britain's consciousness. As self-actualised people, they were not complicit in their subjection through a flawed education system, labour exploitation, the racist criminalisation of Black culture and political exclusion. Instead, some circumvented their conditions and shifting identities through cultural and political empowerment that instilled a sense of pride and self-sufficiency.

In the art world the exposure of non-white British artists was collapsed into a postcolonial or identity-based construction, and the general discourse surrounding their work was tone-deaf and absent of any structural understanding of the unavoidable politics that informed it. The majority of Black artists were marginalised and their work neglected. Indeed, the art world's recognition of many of the artists in this book has been belated and long overdue, and sadly for some of the older artists it arrived too late. Experienced with the kind of contentiousness that greeted Black artists in the UK, Nigerian-British artist Rotimi Fani-Kayode (p.84) once wrote about 'Europeans faced with the dogged survival of alien cultures' and their tendency to act 'as mercantile as they were in the days of the Trade.' Such observers, he continued with disdain, are on a mission to 'sell our culture as a consumer product.'[2]

There can be no denying that the work of Black artists has forced the art world and its audiences to confront some uncomfortable experiences and histories, particularly the legacies of the slave trade, and how British culture and art, and indeed art institutions themselves, have been shaped by it. On its website, Tate tells us, 'Raw sugar imported from the British Caribbean by the Tate or Lyle companies in the post-slavery era would have been from estates established under slavery but worked at that point by wage-labourers and … by indentured labour.'[3] Henry Tate may not have been born until after the abolition of the British Slave Trade, but the generational consequences of centuries of sugar production by enslaved Africans owned as property will always be tied to the land, its raw materials, by-products, and all beneficiaries through primary and secondary markets, even centuries later. And so, the establishment remains incriminated by this association, and by its direct and indirect participation in this history of marginalisation. Ironically or not, the descendants of enslaved canefield workers who harvested and processed the raw material to make the 'white gold' that monied its founder, Henry Tate, are neglected inside the galleries and within the permanent collections.

In more recent times, museums and galleries have made a concerted effort to both exhibit and acquire contemporary and historical works by Black artists. These efforts were furthered by the hugely popular exhibitions such as *Soul of A Nation: Art in the Age of Black Power* (2017), *The Place is Here* (2017) and *Get Up, Stand Up Now: Generations of Black Creative Pioneers* (2019), which idealised a new audience and generated an overwhelming interest in art by Black artists from the general public, students, institutions and the private art sector. These overdue advancements aggregate the possibilities and implications of Black British Art created in the twentieth and twenty-first centuries, and its relationship to other forms of creative production, popular culture and transnational modernisms.

Mainstream arts writing struggles to contextualise Black art, and it often takes a more sociological approach that is overly focused on the artists' racialised personal identity, as opposed to the artworks themselves. And so, it is little wonder that the work of Black British artists has long been relegated to niche status. *A Brief History of Black British Art* is one counteraction that humbly follows the trajectory of writings by cultural observers of Black Britain — most notably critics, essayists and art historians such as Eddie Chambers, Lubaina Himid, Koberna Mercer, Paul Gilroy, Stuart Hall, David A. Bailey and Mark Sealy. In this text I have strung together the ebbs and flows of Black artistic activity in the UK, starting with the pre-Windrush Caribbean Artists Movement of the 1960s before streaming into the Black British Arts movement of the 1980s, and concluding around individual successes despite the isolating Young British Artists' era of the 2000s. My timeline neatly ends with mid-career artists no younger than forty, and so, the younger contemporaries in my own generation are absent. This is a happy conclusion that proves we have a continuing and unique art history robust enough to overflow into multiple books, by multiple authors.

Writing from my position as a British-born Jamaican woman has only enriched and deepened this study of art history. With this book I have attempted to prioritise the form and function of the work, with consideration of non-linear Black cultures, and including the artists' own voices. But this account is not exhaustive. To the surprise of only a few, I have privileged the shadowed profiles of African and Caribbean-descended artists and not 'politically black' practitioners, a categorisation mistakenly popularised in the 1980s by a small minority of artists, activists and academics who did not represent nor consider the lived realities of the wider nation. In spite of this, galleries like Horizon and film collective Retake were established and were rightfully committed to Asian art exclusively. And the Black Art Gallery was founded to represent African and Afro-Caribbean artists exclusively.

Frank Bowling b.1934
Who's Afraid of Barney Newman 1968
Acylic paint on canvas
236.4 x 129.5

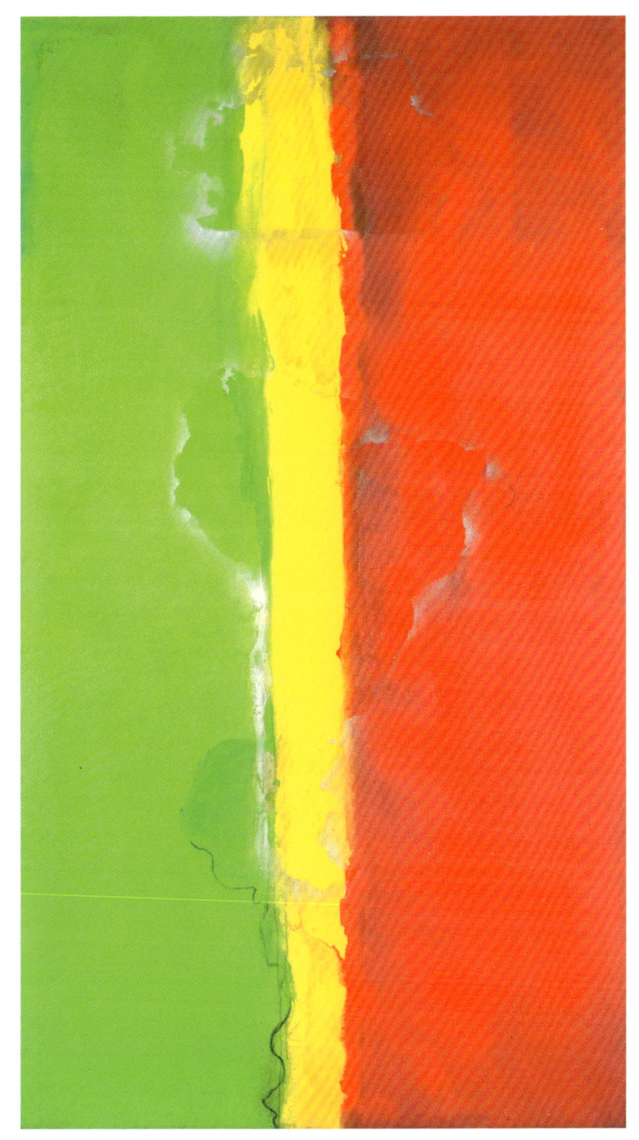

To mangle 'Black' to include Asian and other ethnic minorities, as a nod to some shared experiences of British fascism and colour discrimination, is politically lazy.

To reaffirm Black Britons in the cultural and historical formations of Blackness requires unabashed and corrective storytelling on my part. Racial-smudging for the sake of diversity serves no one, especially Black communities who are still expected to share everything but the burden. We have an already contorted history with minimal recorded perspectives of Black women; racial-smudging into an homogeneous non-white group is fruitless.

Calling the West Indies

Usually omitted from the art-historical timeline is the Caribbean Artists Movement (CAM), an interdisciplinary group who sought to promote and celebrate the work of postwar migrants from British colonies, and to encourage cultural retention. Travelling with the political clamour to advance the goal of self-sovereignty in the West Indies, the writers John La Rose, Kamau Brathwaite and Andrew Salkey founded CAM in 1966.

First meeting in their homes, and later at the Keskidee Arts Centre (Britain's first Black-led arts centre) founded in 1971 in north London, a cabal of novelists, poets, critics, visual artists and historians hosted seminars, workshops, readings and exhibitions, and circulated a newsletter. From 1966 to 1972 members – including the artists Aubrey Williams (p.54), Ronald Moody (p.30), Althea McNish (p.32), Errol Lloyd (p.44) and Paul Dash (p.148), and historian C.L.R. James, novelist Sylvia Wynter, dub poet and activist Linton Kwesi Johnson, and sociologist and theorist Orlando Patterson – would interrogate the connections of their Pan-Caribbean Creole languages, music and literature, and question if there was indeed a 'West Indian Aesthetic'. The surviving legacy of the Caribbean Artists Movement was the activation of a sense of shared Caribbean nationhood outside of their respective home countries, counteracting their reception as unwelcome guests in Britain. Through consciousness-raising groups these cultural producers exchanged ideas that forged a new Caribbean aesthetic in the arts and literature that set the stage for a generation of Black artists in Britain to build upon.

The Crucial Decade

The early 1980s ushered in a politically-charged era; the socio-political upheaval of the Thatcher years (1979 to 1990) saw an outpour of work in response by Black artists in Britain. Far from being an apolitical subjective indulgence, this new emergence of first-generation born and young Black migrants, reshaped the critical debates, political activism, and inevitably the cultural production of the late 1970s and early 1980s.

A good amount of cultural development in this decade was made possible by the economic depression. The now defunct Greater London Council (GLC) actively supported the arts during this time as a way to preoccupy young people, reduce unemployment and to engage with a dissatisfied population. Communities and networks of artists started to come together. On Thursday 28 October 1982, the First National Black Art Convention was accompanied by a four-week exhibition, as a forum for

CALLING ALL BLACK ARTISTS & ART STUDENTS

WE, A GROUP OF BLACK ART STUDENTS BASED IN THE WEST MIDLANDS ARE PLANNING....

THE FIRST NATIONAL BLACK ART CONVENTION

TO BE HELD AT THE FACULTY OF ART AND DESIGN, THE POLYTECHNIC, WOLVERHAMPTON, ON THURSDAY 28th OCTOBER, 1982, FROM 10AM ONWARDS TO DISCUSS THE FORM, FUNCTIONING, AND FUTURE OF BLACK ART.

CONNECTED WITH THIS CONVENTION WILL BE A FOUR WEEK EXHIBITION OF BLACK ART IN THE FACULTY GALLERY. WE NEED BLACK ART STUDENTS AND ARTISTS FROM ACROSS THE COUNTRY TO CONTRIBUTE PIECES OF WORK TO THIS EXHIBITION.

ALL THOSE INTERESTED, PLEASE WRITE FOR FULL DETAILS TO:

KEITH PIPER,
3 LINDSEY WALK,
HYSON GREEN FLATS,
NOTTINGHAM
NG7 6DJ

WITH FINANCIAL ASSISTANCE FROM WEST MIDLANDS ARTS.

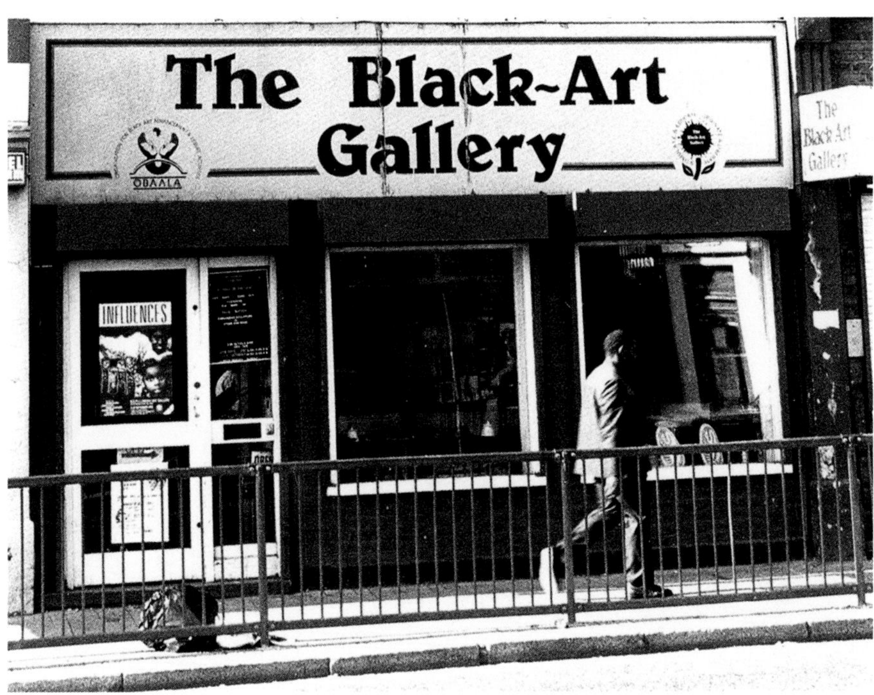

The Black-Art Gallery, 1980s

Original programme for the First National Black Art Convention, October 1982

discussion about 'the form, function, and future of black art.'[4] It was facilitated by a group of determined Black art students at Wolverhampton Polytechnic, known then as the Wolverhampton Young Black Artists. They then became the Pan-Afrikan Connection, and eventually the Blk Art Group, and were both inspired and promoted by the cultural theorist Stuart Hall. Artists associated with the Blk Art Group (mentored by Eric Pemberton, one of their teachers from Lanchester Polytechnic in Coventry) included: Lubaina Himid, Keith Piper, Sonia Boyce, Maud Sulter, Eddie Chambers, Marlene Smith, Donald Rodney, Claudette Johnson, Andrew Hazel, Ian Palmer and Dominic Dawes. Together they went on to be key players

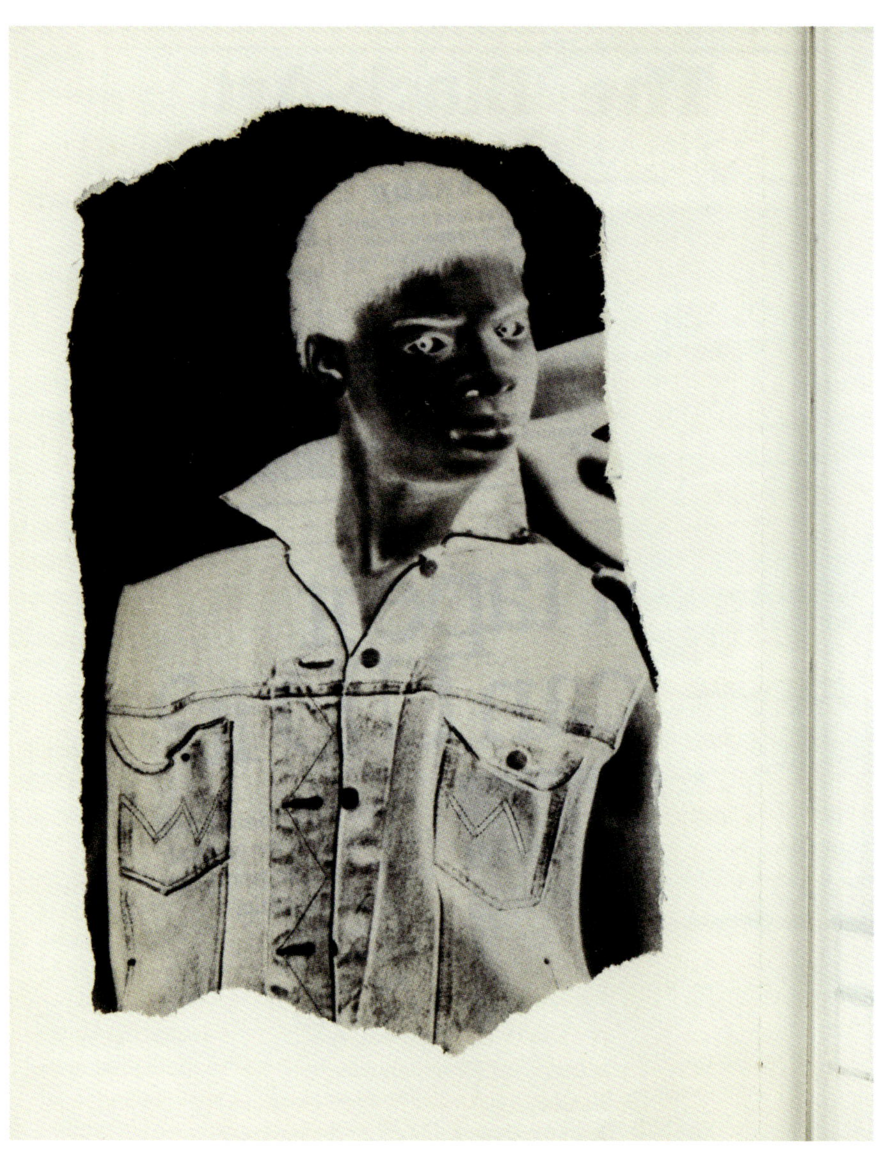

in the 1980s Black Arts Movement (BAM) in the UK at a time of social and political upheaval in Thatcherite Britain, and contested the safety and surveillance of Black communities. With their extended networks, the group began shaping cultural discourse, as well as staging and featuring in key exhibitions, including *Black Art an' done* (1981), *The Other Story* (1989) and, more recently, *Thin Black Line(s)* (2011). Rasheed Araeen's curatorial intervention, *The Other Story* (1989), provided an unprecedented, and personal, overview of postwar modernist practice.

Around the same time, the Black-Art Gallery took shape under the Organisation for Black Arts Advancement and Leisure (later changed to Learning) Activities (OBAALA), and opened in 1982 in Finsbury Park in London, with Shakka Dedi (b.1954) as director. Through the efforts of the gallery, the profile of Black British artists received a major boost by way of visual art presentations, performances and seminars.

The OBAALA manifesto and statement of intent was outlined in the catalogue of its first exhibition *Heart in Exile* (1983), which featured the work of twenty-two artists, all of them of African-Caribbean descent: 'We believe that Black art is born of a consciousness based upon experience of what it means to be an Afrikan descendant wherever in the world we are. "Black" in our context means all those of Afrikan descent and "Art"; the creative expression of the Black person or group based on historical or contemporary experiences. Black-Art should provide an historical document of local and international Black experience. It should educate by perpetuating traditional art forms to suit new experiences and environments. It is essential that Black artists aim to make their art "popular" – that is an expression that the whole community can recognise and understand.'[5]

In November 1982, Channel 4 debuted on British television as the antithesis to the BBC, with a greater emphasis on the needs of minority audiences, and in part a response to the 1981 uprisings in south London, Liverpool, Birmingham, Leeds and Manchester, which were sparked by the hyper-surveillance and brutality of British policing. The Workshop Declaration of 1981, with the backing of Channel 4, the British Film Institute (BFI) and the GLC, supported grant-aided film and video production within the independent film sector. Through this aid, the Black Audio Film Collective, Sankofa Film Collective, and Ceddo Film and Video Workshop (see pp.72, 76 and 78) were founded to counteract the mainstream depictions of Black life. During his interview for the Los Angeles-based magazine, *Black Film Review,* Ceddo filmmaker Menelik Shabazz explained that 'what we have to do is document our history. The uprising(s) this year — for the first time we have a structure where we can go out and, while these events are going on, record them, process them... By documenting events as we are doing, it's laying a tradition and providing an alternative to what has been portrayed in the media. Which has been blatantly racist.'[6]

Slowly, and in small doses, some Black artists became more visible: their work was acquired by museum collections, and they transitioned to the gallery world of representation and the auction house showcases. But insufficient comprehension of their work by white critics did not encourage any serious or lasting dialogue. In the absence of a relationship with the mainstream art world, Black artists often had to exhibit their work in alternative spaces, not specifically dedicated to contemporary art. It was in these restrictive circumstances that Autograph (previously known as the Association of Black Photographers) was 'established in 1988 with the mission of advocating the inclusion of historically marginalised photographic practices.'[7] Following in its wake, the Institute of International Visual Arts (InIVA), from its inception in 1994, dedicated itself to supporting young artists, and mediating between the state policymakers and funding bodies who (unevenly) distribute public monies for creative practices.

Sadly, the existence and survival of these new arts organisations were interwoven with the cultural and temporal politics of arts funding; budget cuts disproportionately affected Black practitioners and still continue to do so. But the value and necessity of Black art should by now be a moot point, and instead the weight and responsibility should remain on those who ignore Black artists and who are reluctant to engage with charged personal histories that are unknown and at times uncomfortable to them.

Who Gets to be a Young British Artist?

The vigorous activity of the 1980s left Black artists exhausted, having spent a decade not only producing artworks, but also acting as agents, exhibition organisers and publishers. In the 1990s, the London-based Young British Artists' (YBA) fame was disseminated abroad, giving the impression of London as a growing and meaningful centre of artistic exchange. But until Tate Modern opened in 2000, London was the only major European city without a public art gallery for modern

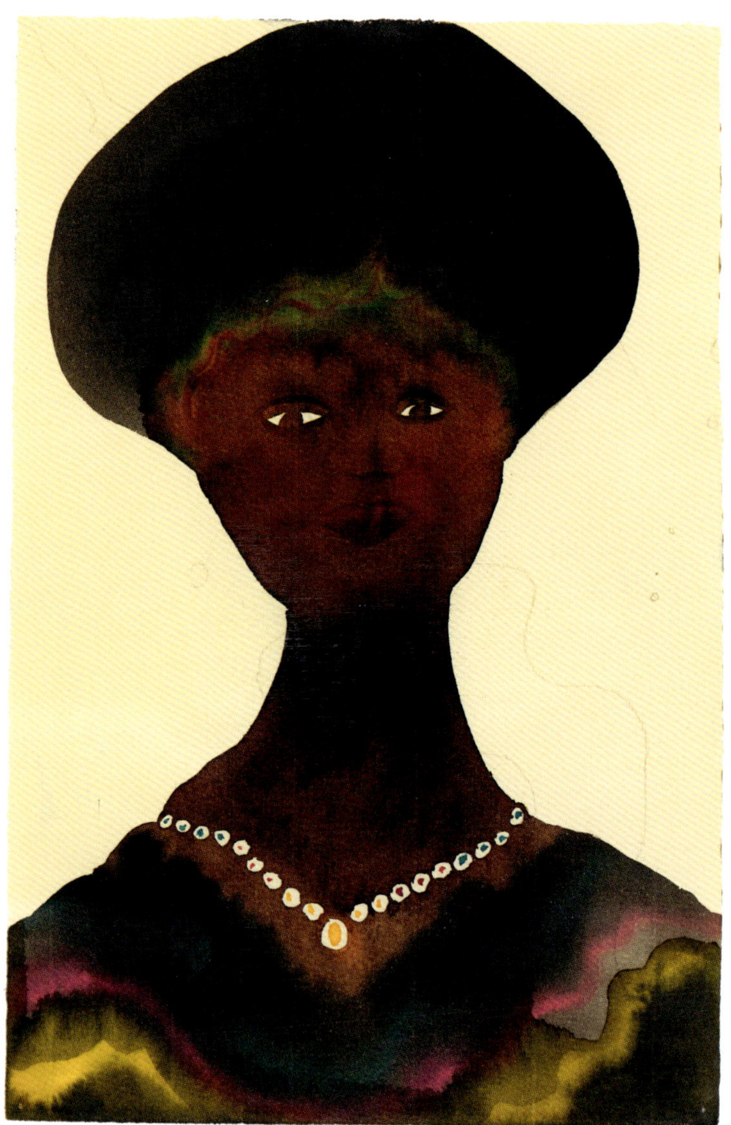

and contemporary art. The inception of a globalised art world may have married with the increased popularity of international fairs and biennales, but it was a world open only to some white and male artists, least of all to anyone in a minority group. Within this period, a handful of Black male artists from the top art schools rose to prominence, including Chris Ofili (the only Black artist considered a member of the YBA group, though the artist himself rejects this categorisation) (p.114) and filmmaker Steve McQueen (p.102), both winners of the Turner Prize, in 1998 and 1999 respectively. But Black artists continued to be marginalised, and Black women artists further still. Eventually, the painter Lynette Yiadom-Boakye (p.122) would find stardom, but only after being well-received in the US. International success is often the marker of progress, and suggests an artist's worthiness for engagement from British art establishments.

Chris Ofili b.1968
Untitled 1998
1 of 30 works on paper;
watercolour and graphite
24 x 15

The New Contemporaries

Today we are bearing witness to artistic enterprise with and without 'white people, white walls, and white wine'[8]. Accessible digital technology, image and text-based social media platforms, such as Twitter and Instagram, and the growing creative capital have provided a much-needed revamp to the unwritten rule book of the largest unregulated market in the world. Our culturally meaningful experiences appear in multiple forms, and visual content and codes migrate from one form to another. In his 1988 essay 'Cruciality and the frog's perspective', cultural critic Paul Gilroy asserts that: 'The issue here is one of priorities, and I think the priority for the black artist is to address Black people. I suppose

if you are realistic and you are concerned with the black
community, you need venues which are located within
and recognised by our own community. I'm aware of all
these problems, but we cannot escape our responsibility
to the community.'[19] But our respective communities
across the four nations (England, Wales, Scotland and
Ireland) are class-ridden, and fumbling with ethnic
antagonisms and other barriers to access.
Meaning, unconsciously or not, we end up prioritising
the importance of certain art forms over others.
The reception for a local documentarist who relies on
independent forums such as Deptford Cinema, for
example, pales in comparison to a high-art film screening
at Tate Modern. The latter is richly stocked by aficionados
and novices alike, invested in the continuation or a
new making of a Black middle class – which is sadly
still heralded as a prominent sign of racial progression.
Displacement through migration, forced or otherwise,
necessitates a constant recreation of cultures and an
affirmation of personhood made from a multiplicity of
layers – as opposed to either/or.

Khadija Saye 1992–2017
Nak Bejjen 2017
Tintype on metal
24.3 × 19.4

Black British Art Today

Given that the basis for art, and therefore aesthetics,
is historically based on Enlightenment values which
prioritise the white European and the male, the reduction
subject of representation is not critical enough to
assess all imbalances. When considered a singular issue,
representation as a form of institutional critique is a
double-edged weapon that allows museum and gallery
practitioners to avoid any considered and professional
judgements on the work of Black artists. Often rendered
unbridgeable, work by Black artists is presented for both

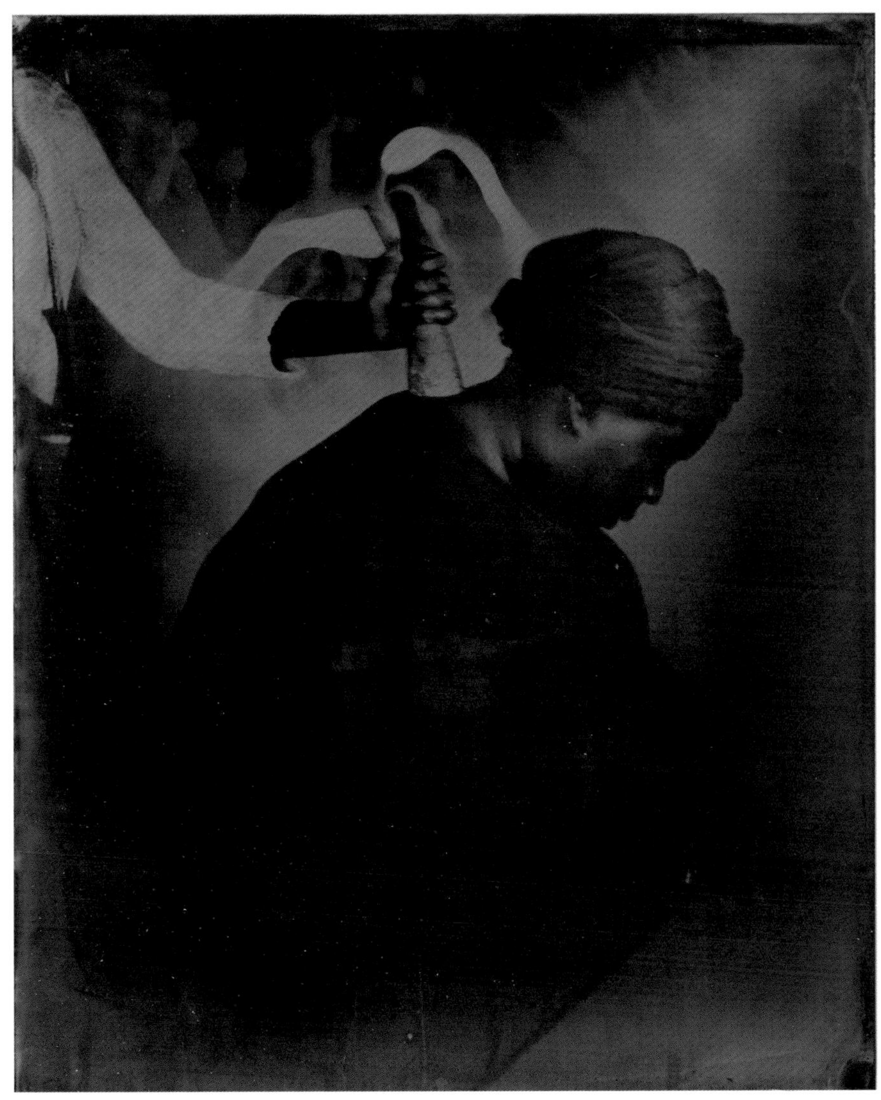

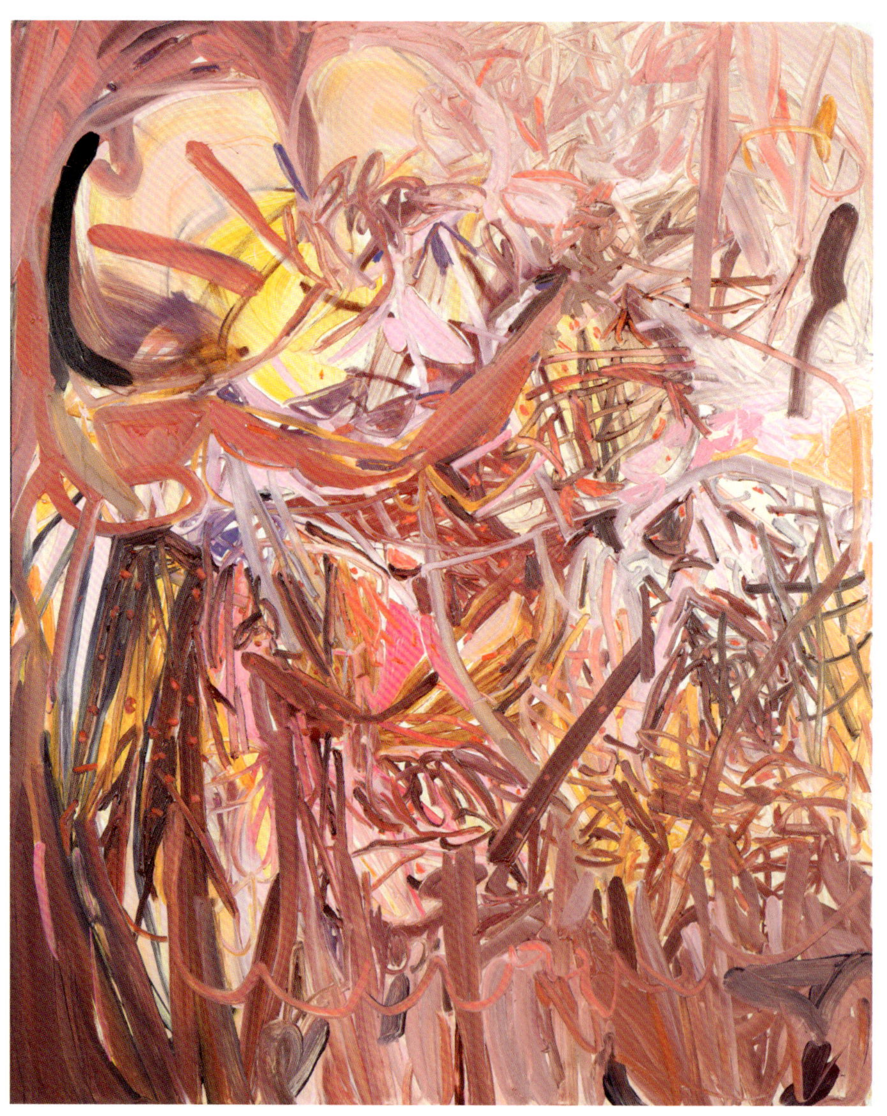

our consumption and contemplation. Hand-selected by directors and senior curators, some Black artists willingly and unwillingly become figureheads of their quick 'progress', while sidelining others.

But with each generation grows a stronger sense of entitlement to occupy British institutions, both educational and cultural. The resilience and resourcefulness of the Black artist is what sustains their practice, but this fact is to be nourished and not exploited. Without a well-funded and malleable infrastructure to support talent for talent's sake, commissioning opportunities remain entangled with tokenism and patronage, leading to pandering that breeds competition and distrust among Black artists. The stakes, for space and status, are high.

Theorist Kobena Mercer offered this reasoning: 'Whether one is making a film, writing a book, organising a conference or curating an exhibition, this "sense of urgency" arises because the cultural reproduction of a certain racism structurally depends on the regulation of Black visibility in the public sphere.'[10] Currently, this 'regulation' is managed and sometimes mismanaged by independent curatorial interventions, collective art-making and nomadic institutions, and steered by Black practitioners and their chosen allies. Simultaneously, scholarship and viewership continue to grow which only allows for a better understanding and argument for the form and function of Black art on a universal but uneven stage.

Jadé Fadojutimi b.1993
I Present Your Royal Highness 2018
Oil paint on canvas
201.5 x 161.1

Works

Ronald Moody 1900–84

A highly-regarded Jamaican sculptor, Ronald Moody gained star status in his home country and in Britain to where he would relocate at the age of twenty-three. Unsatisfied working as a dentist, he formalised his self-taught sculpting practice.

Moody was fixated with the looted Egyptian art on display at the British Museum, London, and almost a year after visiting he had carved the life-sized female head *Midonz,* with shallow cheeks and pronounced lips. The precision and craftsmanship he saw in the ancient Egyptian art is repeated in *Midonz* (also known as Goddess of Transmutation), *Wohin* 1935 and the male counterpart *Tacet* 1938 which make up a trinity of captivating stillness. Moody relocated to Paris, though his stay was cut short and he was forced to leave, two days before Germany invaded France, during the Second World War. The Harmon Foundation, who acquired the sculptures he had to abandon, would not return the work and much to his distress Moody would not see *Midonz* again.

Moody's cultural activity was most prominent in the 1960s, through the exhibitions and conferences of the artists and writers organised by the Caribbean Artists Movement. Speaking about his work in front of the collective he shared, '... the important thing for me, at any rate, was the imagination: in the sense that all our institutions and way of living turn upon an inner source.'[1]

Midonz 1937
Elm
69 x 38 x 39.5

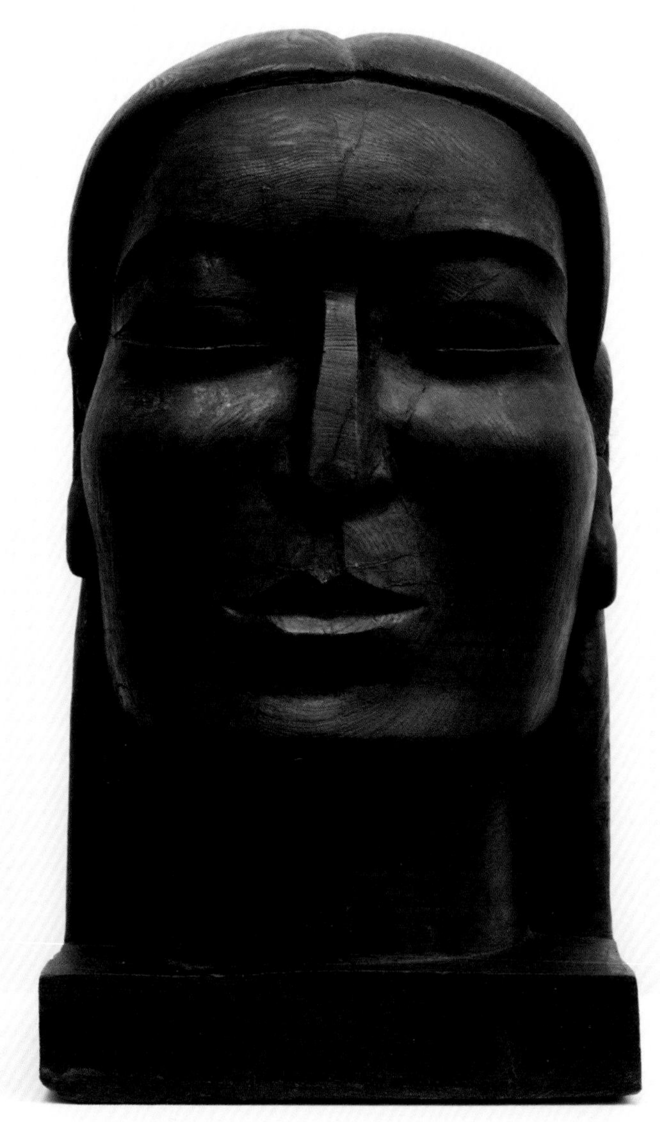

Althea McNish 1924–2020

'Everything I did, I saw it through a tropical eye', is how textile designer Althea McNish defined her practice in 2015.[2] When she arrived in Britain in 1951, the dreariness of the Second World War was embodied in the British monochromatic sense of dress. Taking cues from the tropical vegetation of her birthplace – the colours, light and tints – McNish's designs were a gentle nudge into the Swinging Sixties.

McNish's first interview as a graduate was with the London department store Liberty, in 1959, where she was offered a job in the first meeting. She was one of the first Black designers of the 1960s to establish a significant international appeal. She was frequently commissioned to create original domestic textiles, and by fashion design manufacturers, including couture fashion house Dior. She also designed fabrics for the official wardrobe of Queen Elizabeth II, for her state visit to Trinidad. Though McNish's designs were sometimes abstract, and occasionally geometric, much of her work draws on nature. Her first commercial design, *Golden Harvest,* pictured here, was inspired by a visit to the botanical Essex countryside. It became the Whitworth Gallery's best-selling design and was still being manufactured into the 1970s.

Alongside Aubrey Williams (1926–90), McNish was a key member of the Caribbean Artists Movement in the 1960s, and participated in the ongoing articulation of Caribbean art.

Golden Harvest 1959
Screenprint on cotton
143 x 127

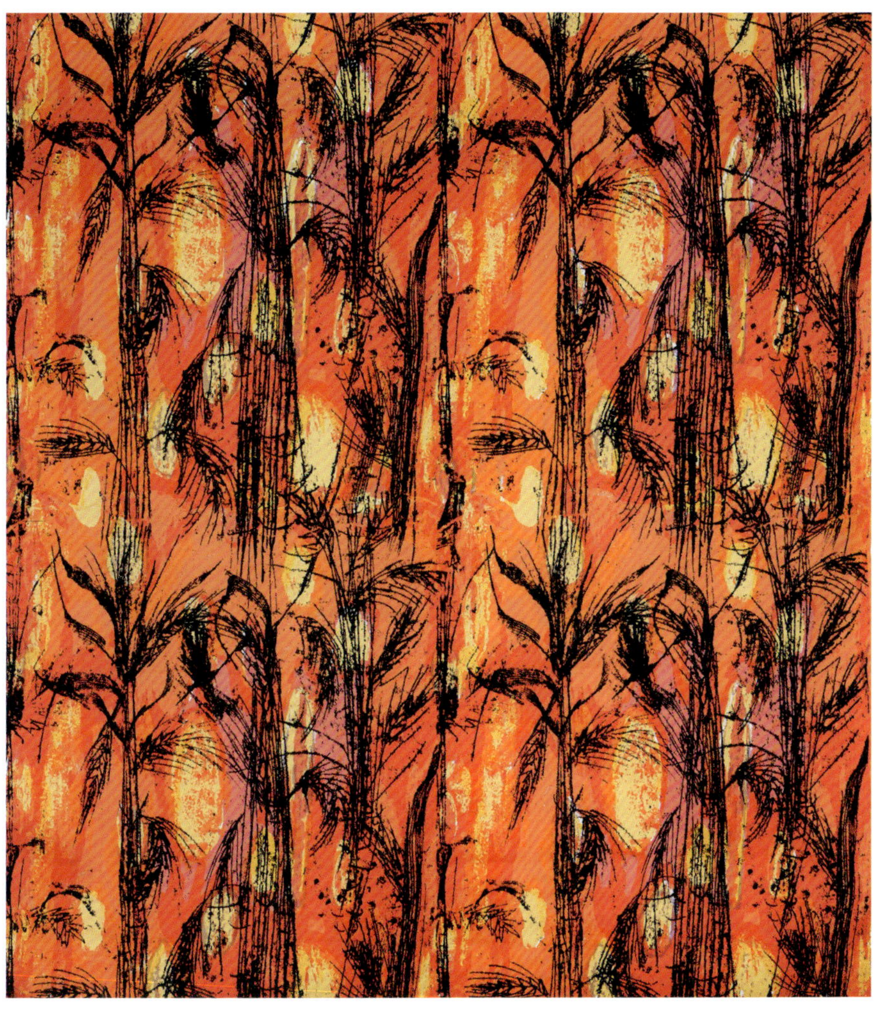

Frank Bowling b.1934

Untitled (Mother's House) features the screenprinted image of Frank Bowling's mother, in front of her small dressmaking business in his birthplace, Guyana, where he worked part-time as a young boy.

Now famous for his abstract, paint-pouring inventions, in his earliest years of experimentation, Bowling experimented widely with figuration and screenprinting techniques, and linked colour-field painting and stenciling to reconstruct personhood through and despite migration. On a scholarship, Bowling graduated from the Royal College of Art in 1962, with classmates David Hockney and Allen Jones (both b.1937) – soon to be spearheads of British Pop Art. Bowling was expected to win the Gold medal for painting, but instead came second place to Hockney. Later, in 1965, curator Bryan Robertson plainly told the artist, 'England is not ready for a gifted artist of colour.'[3]

In the 1960s Bowling maintained a studio and residence in London, near Tate Britain, as well as a studio in New York. Taking a keen interest in abstract art, he migrated to New York in 1966 at the peak of the Black Art Movement. There he found camaraderie with Black American artists who mirrored his talent and subject matter. Bowling was staunch in his resistance to the perceived limitations of Black figurative art, writing criticism for *Art News*, and the *Arts Magazine* where he was contributing editor between 1969 and 1972.

Untitled (Mother's House)
1966
Oil paint and screenprinted
ink on two stapled
canvases 119.7 × 79.1

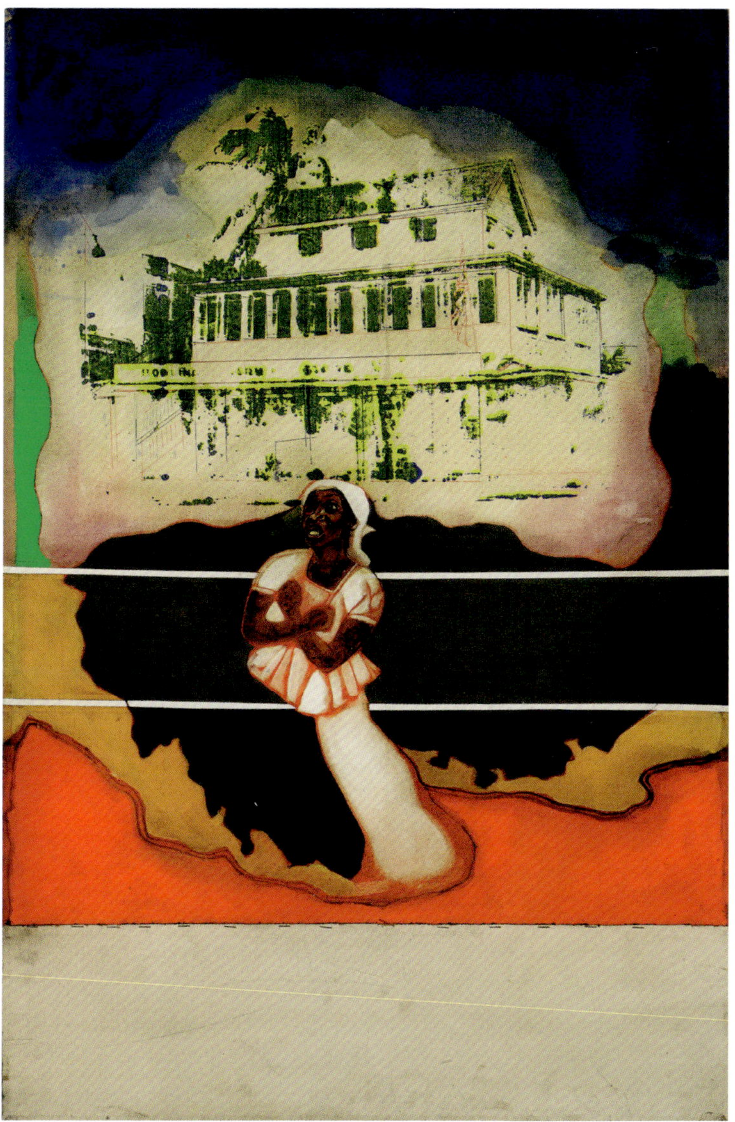

Uzo Egonu 1931–96

The printmaker and arguably 'Africa's greatest'[4] painter, Uzo Egonu, left Nigeria as a teenager already experienced with paint. Egonu lived in England but was able to maintain links with his peers through the West Africans Students Union in London. His close friendship with Ronald Moody (p.30), despite their thirty-year age difference, would see him become heavily involved with the Caribbean Artists Movement, and later establish a parallel group for Africans. Egonu took up residency in multiple European cities: Denmark, Finland, Italy and Paris, but his practice was modernist by way of Africa and not Europe.

Woman in Grief takes a geometric form. Painted on canvas, a representational female figure is fractionated and contorted, made in the same year as the two Battles of Onitsha in Nigeria (the artist's place of birth) the painting serves as a commemoration of the political times and the effects on his fellow countrymen. Historian Olu Ouguibe formulated that for 'Egonu it was only proper that African artists should not lose themselves in the fiction of a universalist modernism. Instead, they should define a place for themselves within modernism whilst also registering the specificities of their origins.'[5]

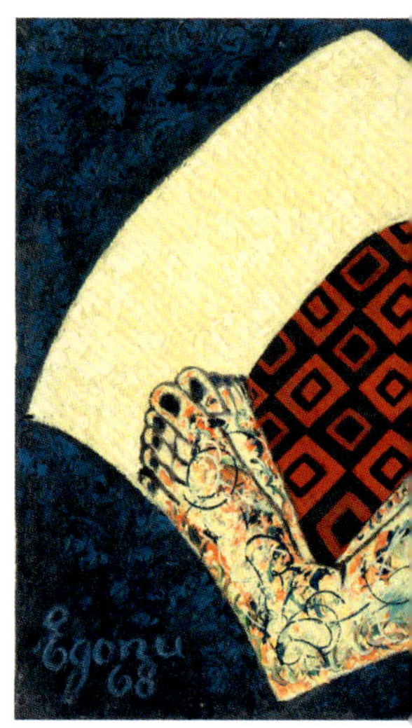

Woman in Grief 1968
Oil paint on canvas
48.2 x 120.2

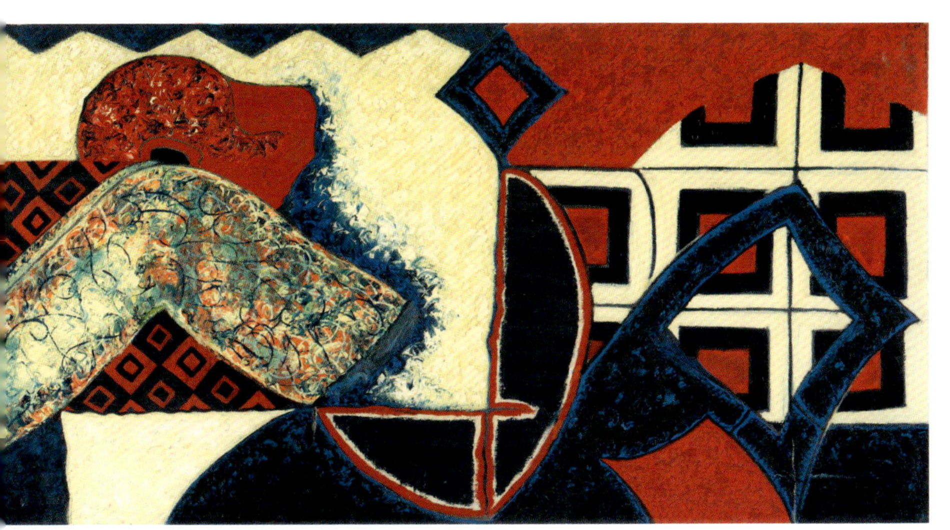

Horace Ové b.1939

Windrush Generation is Horace Ové's still capture of his first and closest community in Britain. An older Black man and woman flirt with the music and passersby on the streets of Notting Hill, in celebration of the carnival as practised in the Caribbean. Carnival is most famously associated with Trinidad, Ové's place of birth, but uniquely varies from island to island.

Ové is best known as the first Black British filmmaker to direct a feature-length with the 1975 film *Pressure*. Chronicling three generations of a Trinidadian family in west London, and the political radicalisation of Black youth, the film was banned for two years by the British Film Institute, its funder. In a 1987 issue of the *Monthly Film Bulletin,* Ové offers more context: 'Here in England there is a danger, if you are Black, that all you are allowed to make is films about Black people and their problems. When things happen here, like Broadwater Farm or the Brixton riots, I get very annoyed with the media coverage. It is so superficial. They don't do proper research. That is why I made *Pressure*. I was tired of reading in the papers about young Blacks hanging around on street corners, mugging old ladies. Nobody tried to find out why they were doing it.'[6]

Windrush Generation 1969
35mm colour transparency
film, printed on paper
40.6 x 50.8

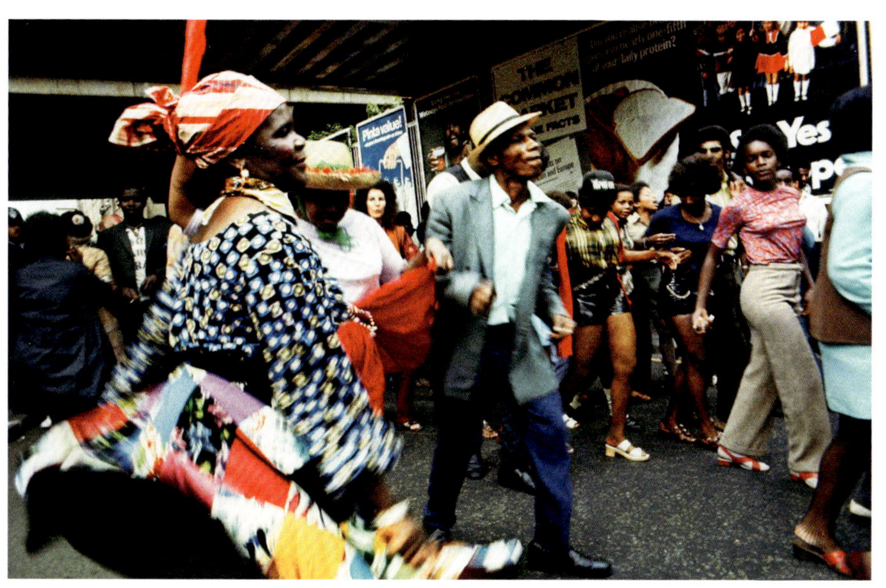
Pinta value!
THE
COMMON
MARKET
THE FACTS
Yes

Donald Locke 1930–2010

Trophies of Empire is an installation of assorted phallic- (presumably imperial) bullets, sitting in various vessels – a candle holder, a chalice or leather-bound chains – and displayed in an open, shelved cabinet. In a letter to a Tate curator, shortly before he passed away, Donald Locke explained: 'The cylindrical shapes are "bullets" but I have had to accept that very few people read them this way. In the old days in British Guyana [sic.], athletic meetings were big events with prizes given in the form of a cup or trophy, a shiny metal goblet mounted on a black, wooden base. It was a thing of great value to the winner.'[7]

The bottom row of 'trophies' features assemblages made by Locke's students at the boys' school and detention home, Hammersmith House in London, where he taught poetry. This intergenerational participatory element and the visual research informing his art-making, is but one testament to Locke's ability to balance a history of capture and a future of control.

Trophies of Empire 1972–4
Ceramic, wood, metal, glass and other materials
190.5 x 129.5 x 20.3

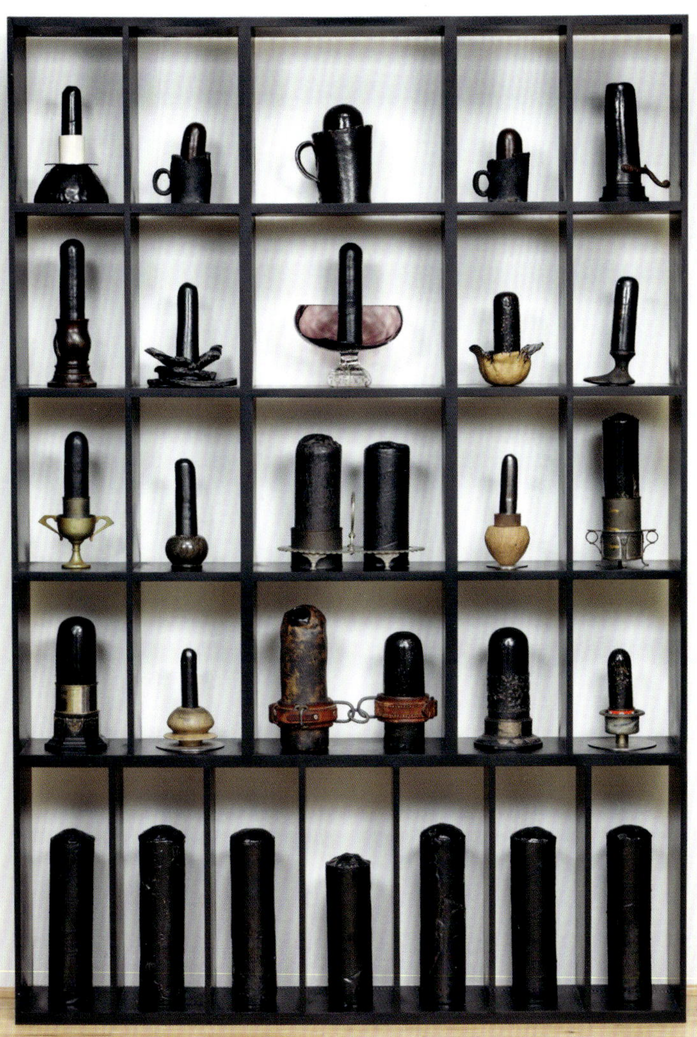

Raphael Albert 1935–2009

After settling in West London, Grenada-born Raphael Albert would host Black beauty pageants from the 1960s to the 1980s, mostly targeted at women from the British-Caribbean community. Albert's photographs of the 'Miss Black and Beautiful', 'Miss West Indies in Great Britain' and 'Miss Grenada' beauty pageants constitute an archive of Black British style and sensuality.

Hearing the global chant of 'Black is beautiful', Black women were defining the parameters of their femininity within a British context, but outside of their white Western ideals. In the still *Miss Black & Beautiful* illustrated here, pageant winner Sybil McLean smiles, her new title draping across her torso and her crown sitting atop her cropped baby afro, as her fellow contestants brush her cheeks with congratulatory kisses. What comes across in Albert's photographs, beyond the women's beauty, is their collective celebration of Afro-Caribbean womanhood, self-actualisation and self-fashioning.

Miss Black & Beautiful
Sybil McLean with
fellow contestants
(Patricia Livingston left),
Hammersmith Palais,
London 1972, printed 2012
Gelatin silver print on
paper 28.1 x 27.6

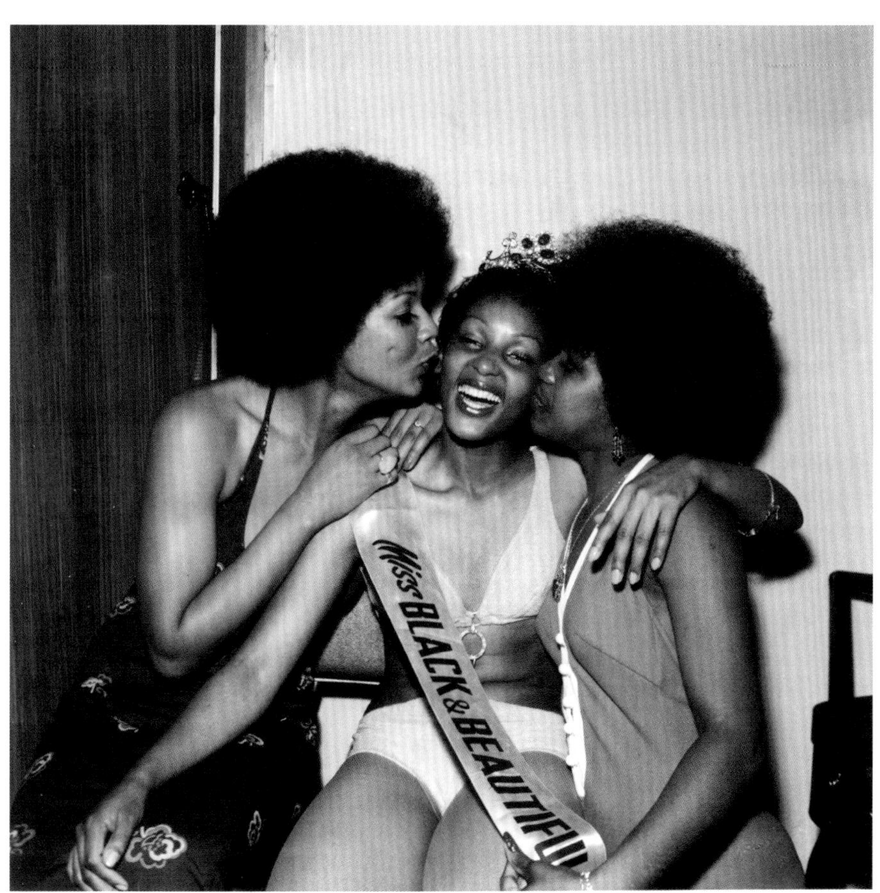
Miss BLACK & BEAUTIFUL

Errol Lloyd b.1943

'You can't entirely ignore your environment. If you live in England it is very difficult to deal with West Indian problems all of your life. Personally, if I could paint in the way that Sparrow sings calypso, I'd be very happy.'[8]

Jamaican-born Errol Lloyd was interested in faces, which appear in many of his paintings, illustrations and sculptures. Mostly self-taught, Lloyd worked in isolation in London until he joined the Caribbean Artists Movement (CAM) in 1967 as one of the group's youngest artists.

New Beacons Books, the bookstore of CAM's founding member, John La Rose, served as the primary site of organisation for the artists, but also for the Black Parents Movement, and the supplementary education for Black children in the 1970s and 1980s. Keskidee Arts Centre was Britain's first Black arts centre founded in 1971, with an emphasis on cultural education and activity. Its co-founder instated Lloyd as their first artist-in-residence. *The Lesson* perfectly exemplifies the principles of Keskidee: a young boy sits on the floor with a blackboard and chalk in hand, overseen by an elder.

The Lesson 1972
Oil paint on canvas
76 x 61

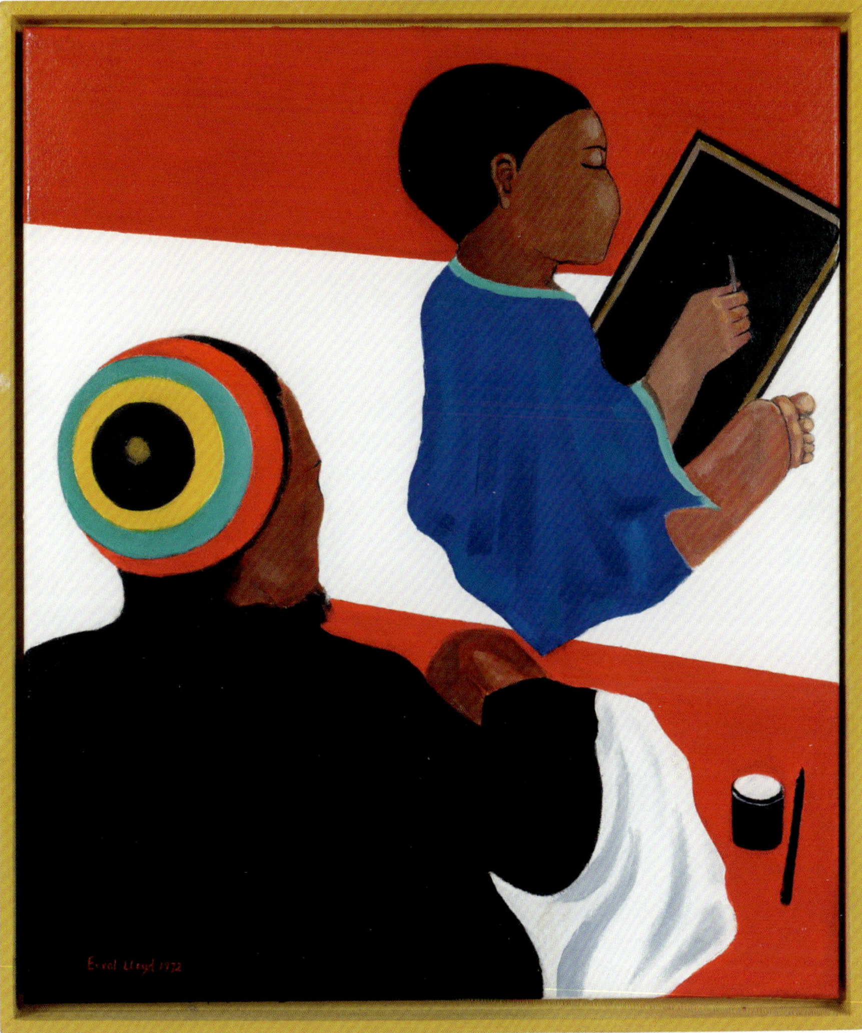

Neil Kenlock b.1950

From 1968 until 1973, the British Black Panther movement operated in Brixton, south London. At this time, self-taught Neil Kenlock would become their official photographer. *Demonstration Outside Brixton Library* was a common scene. When hundreds gathered outside the US embassy to protest the treatment of Black Americans and to support the global struggle for emancipation, Jamaican-born Kenlock was in the midst with his camera.

High unemployment, the rise of far-right groups such as the National Front, inadequate housing, social exclusion, 'sus' laws (a precursor to 'stop and search') and state violence in the UK prompted calls for the disenfranchised group to radically mobilise themselves. Kenlock also recorded the mass demonstration in 1970 that led to the court case of the Mangrove Nine, a group of Black British activists charged for inciting a riot at the protest against racial harassment by the police. The group were so-called because of the particular police targeting of The Mangrove, a Caribbean restaurant in Notting Hill, west London. Fifty-five days later the members of the group were finally acquitted and forced the first judicial acknowledgment that there was 'evidence of racial hatred' in the Metropolitan police. Kenlock memorialised the trial with detailed and intimate photographs of otherwise overlooked communities.

Demonstration Outside Brixton Library 1972, printed 2010
Gelatin silver print on paper 38.3 x 25.3

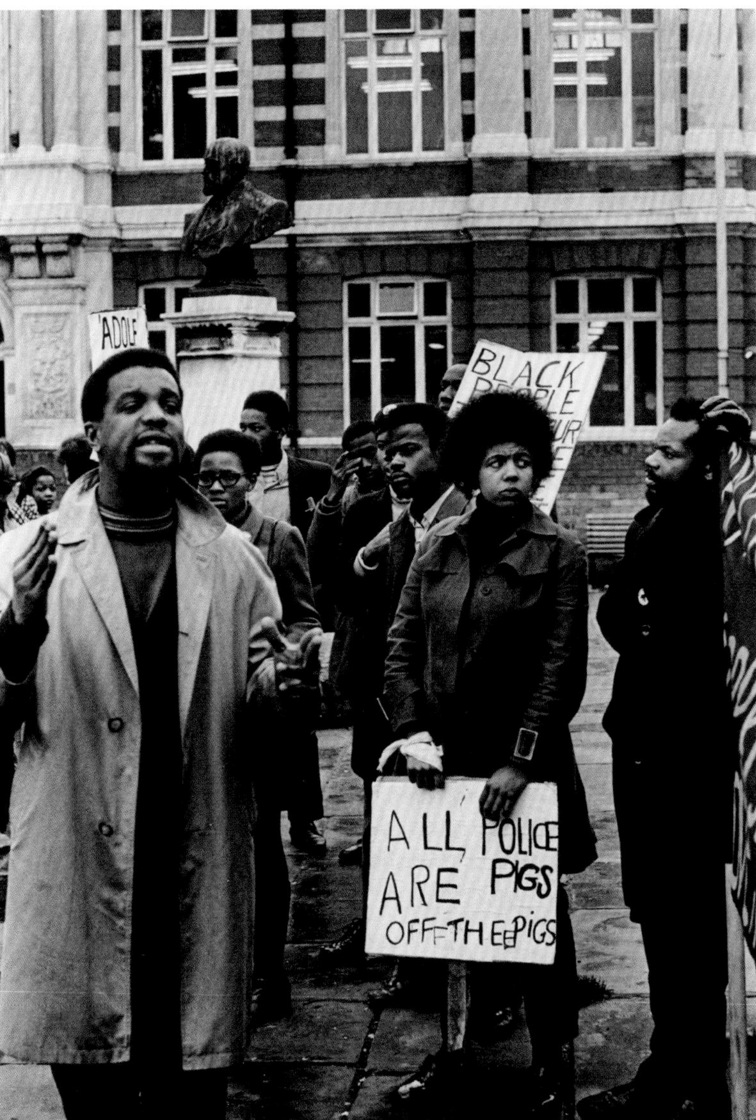
'ADOLF
BLACK
PEOPLE
ALL POLICE
ARE PIGS
OFF THE PIGS

Charlie Phillips b.1944

This image captures a flash moment where a bereaved gravedigger takes a brief pause to address both the physical and emotional exertion of the task. He is Andrew Shervington, a community leader in Notting Hill during the race riots in 1958.

Charlie Phillips's photo is one of a series dedicated to the traditions that surround death and mourning in London's Black Caribbean community, especially that known as Nine Nights. As evidenced in the name, Nine Nights refers to the nine days leading up to a funeral, during which feasting and communion in the name of the honoured take place across various homes. On the ninth night, the spirit (or 'duppy' in Jamaican patois, and as it is known in Phillips's place of birth) leaves the physical body in time for the ceremony and burial the following day. This life-cycle ritual continues today.

The photographer asserts: 'A Caribbean funeral is not just about burial, it's about celebration as well. You celebrate a week before, a week after and a year later when you have the remembrance. You can see some of the etiquette, like the dogs and horse-drawn carts and all that. Some of the traditional songs like "How Great Thou Art" was a typical theme song for African Caribbean funerals.'[9]

Whilst Red closed the grave at Sammy Coteys funeral the mourners sing, from the series *How Great Thou Art* 1973 Gelatin silver print on paper 61 x 55

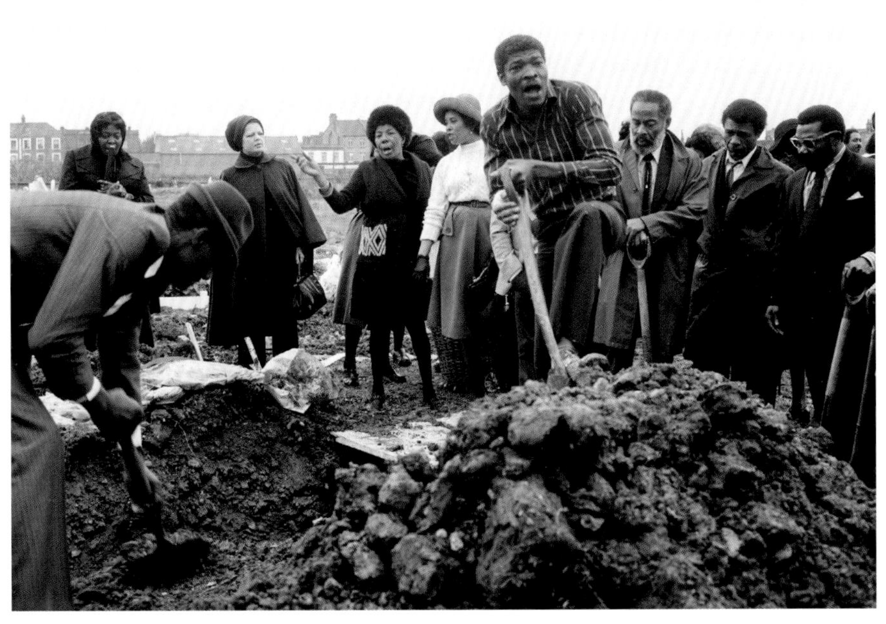

Winston Branch b.1947

In 1966, at the age of fifteen, Winston Branch left St Lucia for Britain, where his family figured it would be best for him to study and become a working artist. Once there, Branch developed his painting practice at the Slade School of Fine Arts, and then at the British Academy in Rome, before obtaining a Guggenheim Fellowship in 1978.

West Indian is a contrast to Branch's typically abstract work, in which a well-styled Black man, donning a brown coat and bobbled hat, is framed by yellow and green vertical coloured blocks, centring him within what could be the opening doors of a train. Witnessing a scene of merriment among friends on a train to Hamburg, Branch relays the motivation behind the portrait: 'It's very interesting to think about, living in a turbulent time of immigrants, and migration. I went with a friend on a Friday, and I saw all these young Black men, handsome, beautiful, semi-drunk, at the train station. And they were huddled together. And I asked my friend, "why are these Black people, where are they going and why are they drunk?", and they said "well, they are kind of having a nostalgic epiphany, of going back home."'[10]

West Indian 1973
Oil paint on canvas
105 x 90.2

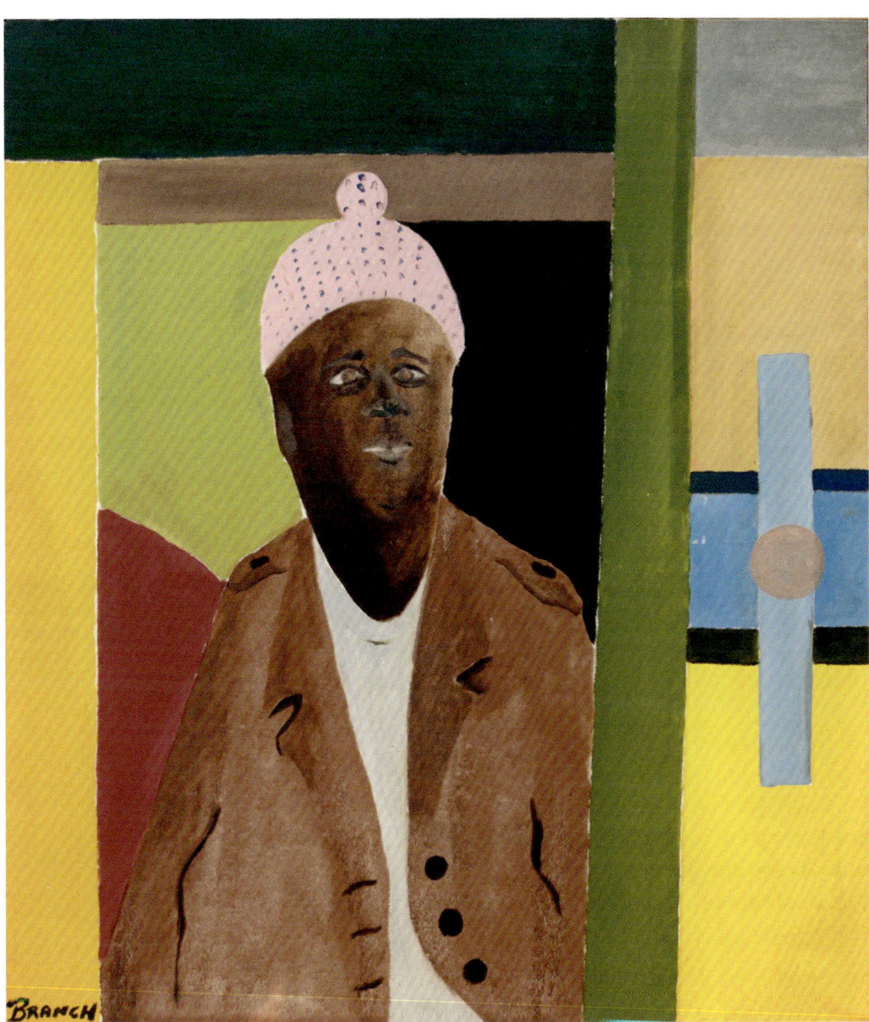

BRANCH

Dennis Morris b.1960

Soul Sister shows a young Black girl gusto enough to pose for a photograph wearing two pairs of, now retro, sunglasses which bridge the gap between her forehead and afro. With her palms clasped and resting against her chin, she is resolute and without a smile. Dennis Morris reflects: 'There was a series of events, which were very influential on my generation. Early in the 1970s came Shaft (1971) and Superfly (1972) movies, and Roots the TV series followed in 1977. This was the first time that we as young kids had been exposed to our history. It was captivating and inspiring. I started taking different photos of my friends and surroundings. I began to see differently and took photographs showing Black strength, pride, style and cool.'[11]

Arriving in London from Jamaica as a young boy, Morris, like many others in the country, was stirred by the rise of Bob Marley and Reggae music in Britain. Upon learning that Marley would be arriving in the UK for the first time, Morris skipped school and waited outside the Speakeasy where Marley was to appear to eventually ask the singer, 'Can I take your picture?'. Endeared by the aspirational fourteen-year old Morris, Marley quickly granted his access and invited him to follow him on the rest of his UK tour. By the age of sixteen, Morris would create some of the most reproduced images of Bob Marley to date.

Soul Sister, Hackney 1974
Gelatin silver print on paper 61 x 50.8

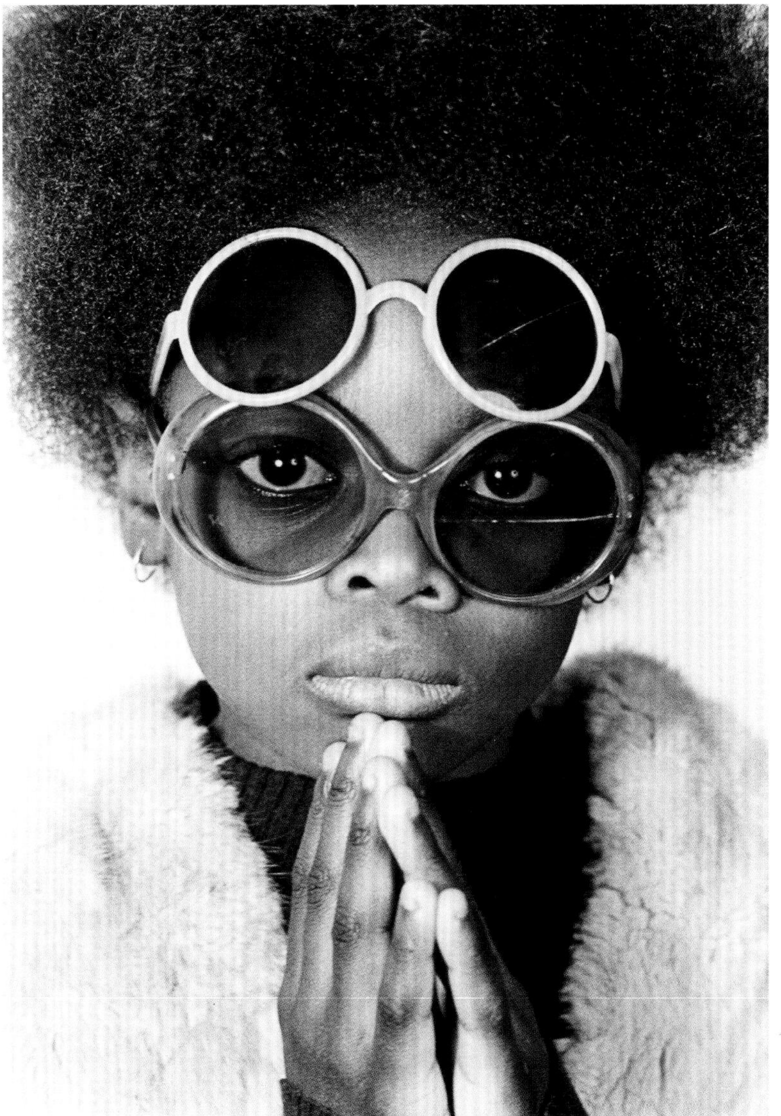

Aubrey Williams 1926–90

As an early and mature member of the Caribbean
Artists Movement (CAM), frequently invited to exhibit
in Paris, Milan and Chicago, Guyanese-born painter
Aubrey Williams convened at the London flat of Jamaican
socialist Orlando Patterson (b.1940) in January 1967
to collectively question the 'West Indian aesthetic'.
Patterson's first novel *The Children of Sisyphus* was
published soon after to a great reception, lauded for
its humanising social-realist narration of excluded
Rastafarians in Jamaica.

In the 1970s, Williams was making large canvases
between studios in Florida and Jamaica, and was by then
best known for his homages to the Amerindian natives
of Guyana, and their artistic practices. *Painting of a man
wearing a Rastafarian hat* is a further illustration of his
respect for folk wisdom and ancestral intuition in the
portrait head and shoulders of a Rastaman donning
his red, green and gold tam. Articulating his hope for
Caribbean art, Williams believed 'the forces meeting
in the Caribbean and all around the archipelago will
eventually, I feel, change this world… not in the sense
of a big civilisation in one spot, but as the result of
the total of man's experience and groping for the
development of his consciousness.'[12]

Painting of a man wearing a
Rastafarian hat 1977
Oil paint on canvas
45.3 × 30

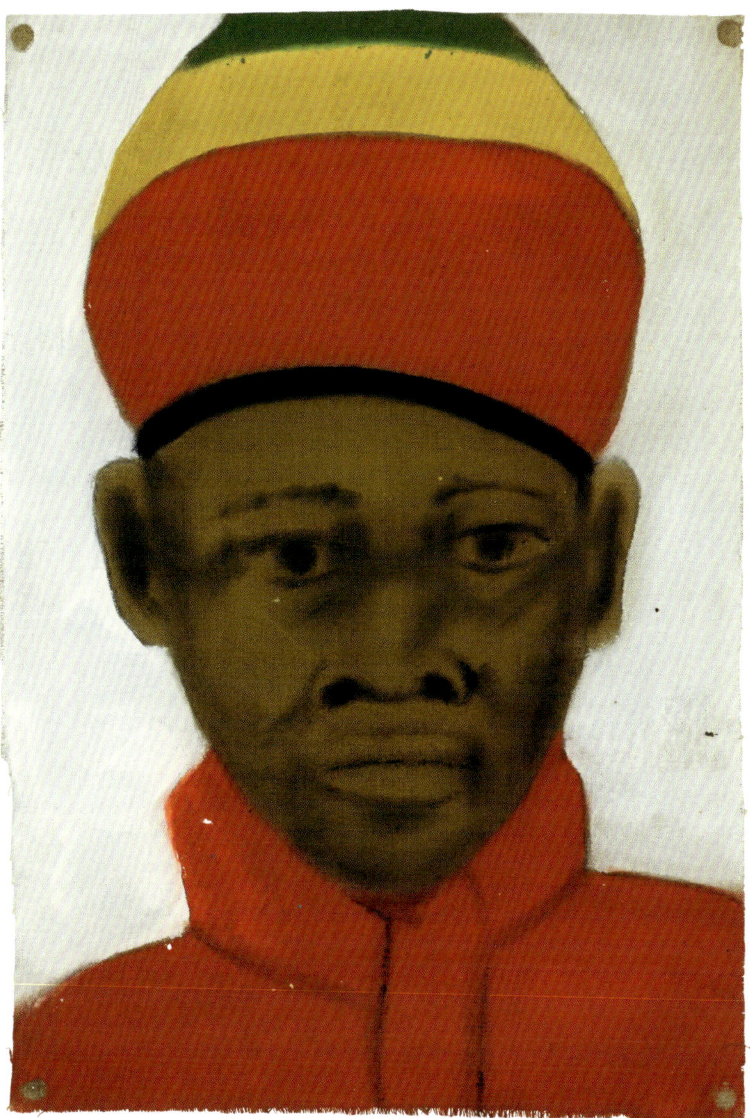

Vanley Burke b.1951

Vanley Burke moved from Jamaica to Birmingham in 1965, already acquainted with the camera gifted to him on his tenth birthday. Birmingham's Handsworth Park was the site of Burke's most impressive piece of photography: *African Liberation Day.* For this special event, he bought ten rolls of film to bear witness to the hundreds of Black youths gathered together, with their crowns and afros uniformly facing the stage and speakers.

In a special BBC Radio 4 documentary, *Face in the Crowd,* Burke shared: 'There weren't any white people in the park, there were no policemen, either. It was just full of Black people and it was strange to have that and it was also quite exhilarating to see that so many people could have come out for a cause and support for a wider community.'[13]

This is one of a hundred black-and-white photographs taken over forty years that make up Burke's photo collection *Rivers of Birminam,* previously described as the 'greatest photographic document of Caribbean people in post-war Britain.'[14]

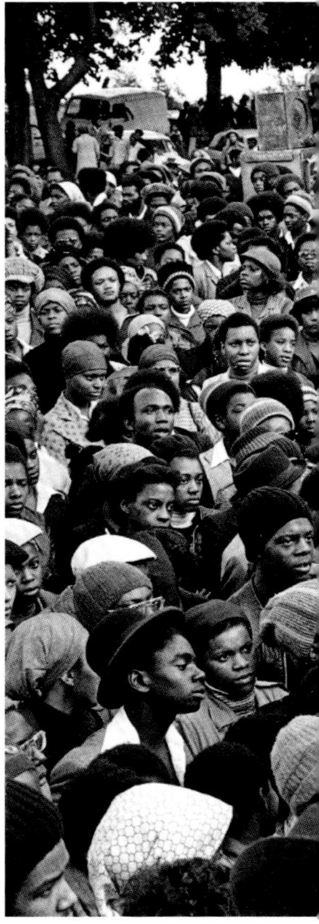

Africa Liberation Day Rally in Handsworth 1977
Gelatin silver print on
paper 30.5 x 40.6

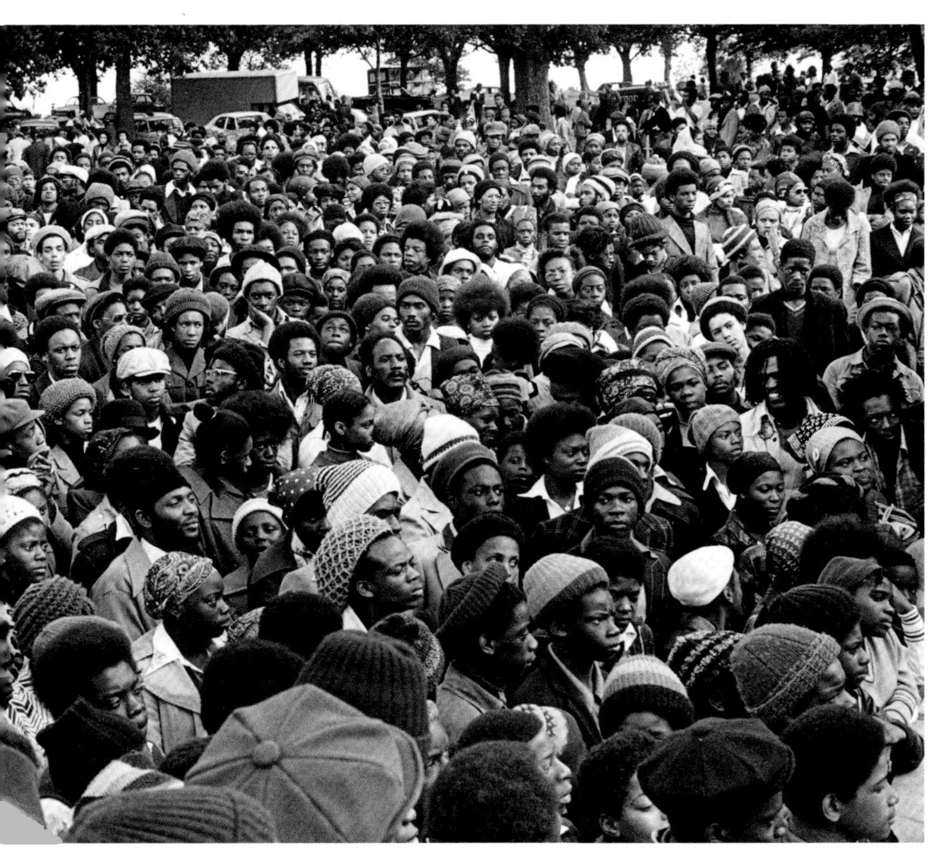

Eddie Chambers b.1960

Eddie Chambers was a leading figure of the Blk Art Group, and much like the other artists in the collective, he was sharp and confrontational. His best-known work, *Destruction of the National Front* illustrates the fragmented Union Jack and the swastika. With Jamaican parentage, violent hostility from British fascists towards early Black migrants could be easily recounted by Chambers and his British-born generation. Concurrent to exhibiting his art, Chambers curated several important shows including *Black Art: Plotting the Course* in 1988 and *Black People and the British Flag* in 1993. He has published essays, reviews and books that remain quintessential for any reader of contemporary Black art.

In the catalogue for the 1983 exhibition *The Pan-Afrikan Connection* in Nottingham, Chambers wrote: 'Black art, at the very least, should indicate and/or document change. It should seek to affect such change by aiming to help create an alternative set of values necessary for better living, stronger communities, contemporary cultural identity and so on… rather than merely reflecting the moral bankruptcy of modern times, as does the majority of white art. (…) Black art, like everything else in the Black community, must respond positively to the urgent reality of revolution. Very necessary revolution.'[15]

Destruction of the National Front 1979–80
4 screenprints on paper on card
82.7 × 57.2 each

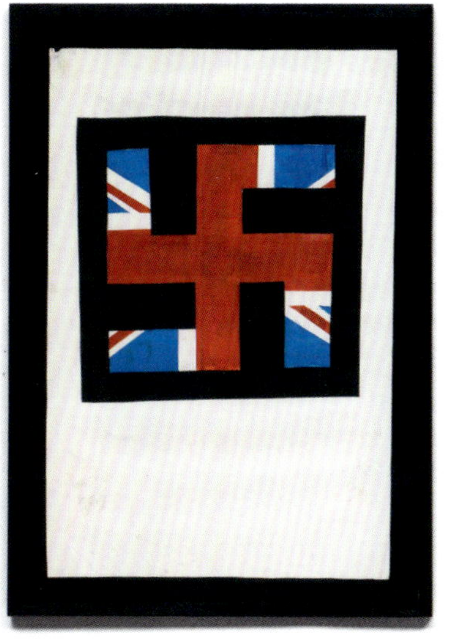 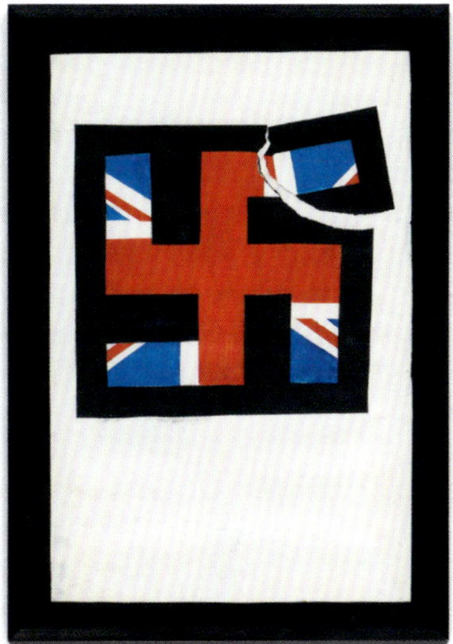

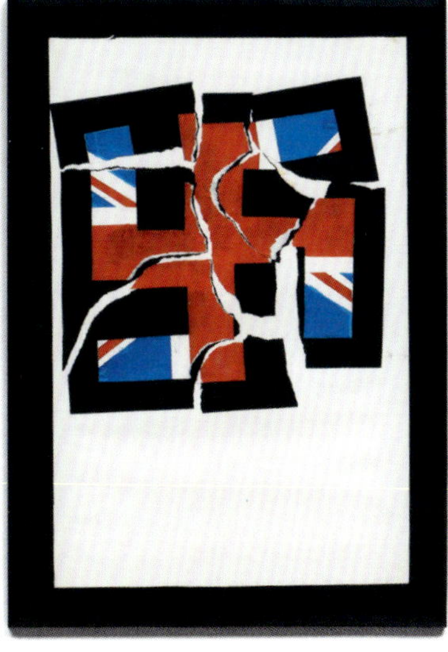 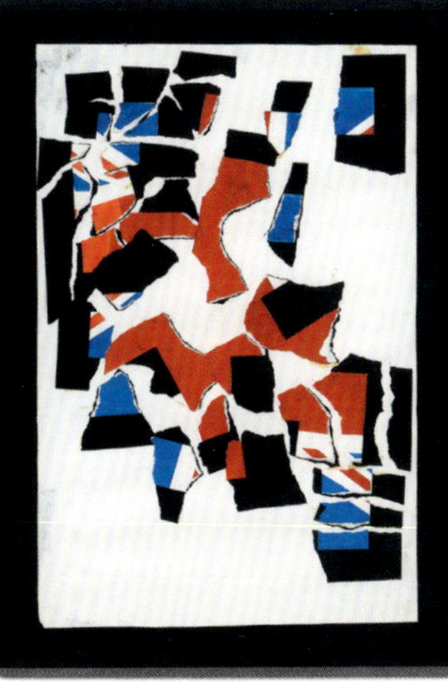

Armet Francis b.1945

First working in advertising and fashion photography in England, Armet Francis would eventually turn to capturing Black local histories. At the time Francis was working, not all immigrants were embraced by churches in the UK forcing communities to establish their own. Churches were one of the few private spaces in Britain that Black people could comfortably inhabit. *Black Church* is a black-and-white rendering of first row worshippers, in black berets and Sunday white bow lapel shirts. Each woman is sitting upright fixated on opposing angles of the room, but never at the camera.

This photograph is just one of the images that make up Francis's *Roots to Reckoning* archive – a collection of ninety photographs of London's early Black communities taken between the 1960s and the 1980s. *The Black Triangle,* his first documentary collection of the global African diaspora, was initiated in 1969 and displayed at his solo exhibition at the Photographers' Gallery in 1983. Francis was the first Black photographer to have a solo exhibition at the Gallery.

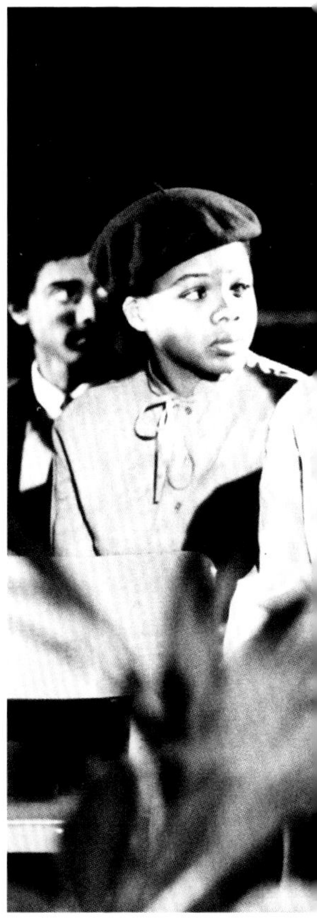

Black Church 1980
Gelatin silver print
on paper

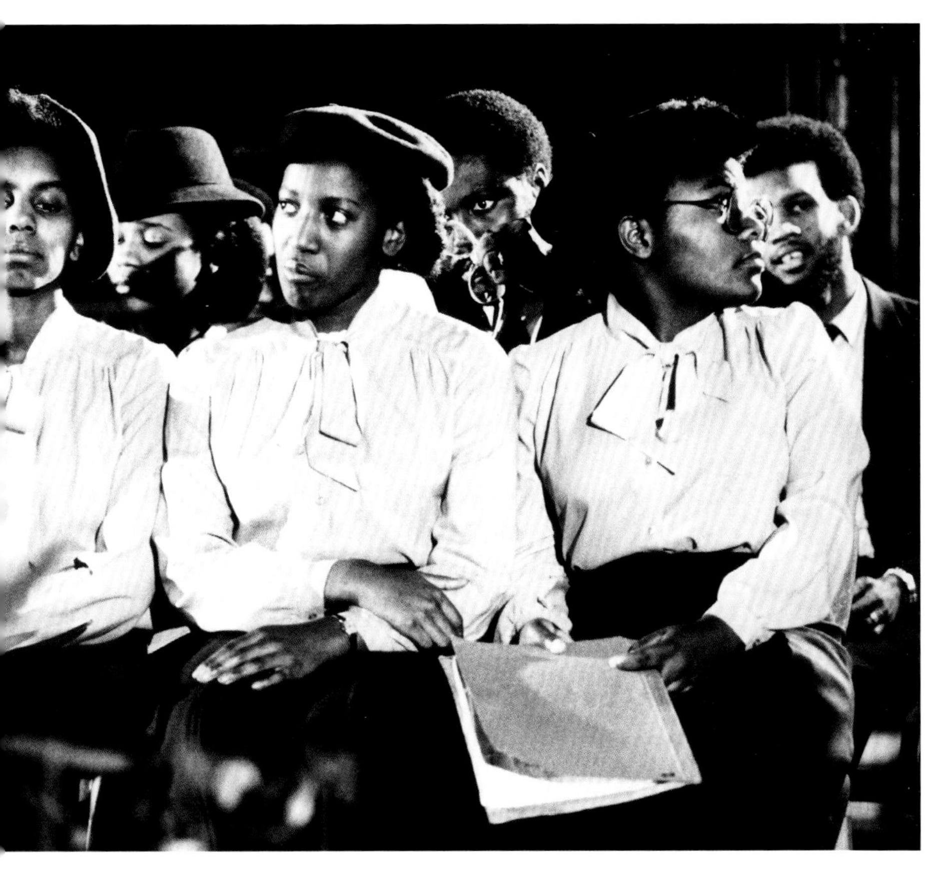

Menelik Shabazz 1954–2021

Burning an Illusion was directed by a founding member of the Ceddo Film and Video Collective, the Barbados-born Menelik Shabazz. Fewer than a handful of films feature a Black British woman as both a lead actor and love-interest. Cassie McFarlane plays the newly independent Pat, living solo in Notting Hill and working in an office, until a fitting suitor, Del, enters the picture.

When speaking of this debut feature-length film Shabazz revealed: 'I was motivated by the need to address our identity through a tale of love. When the lead character Pat burns her illusions, she rejects notions of idyllic love but most importantly she burns a false identity of self. This self was trapped in embracing ideas and culture that was not her own. When the gap between her reality and Mills and Boon's world becomes apparent, her love life in tatters, her boyfriend in prison – she is forced to confront herself. She finds a new way of seeing, embraces her African roots, symbolic of her transition and sense of self.'[16]

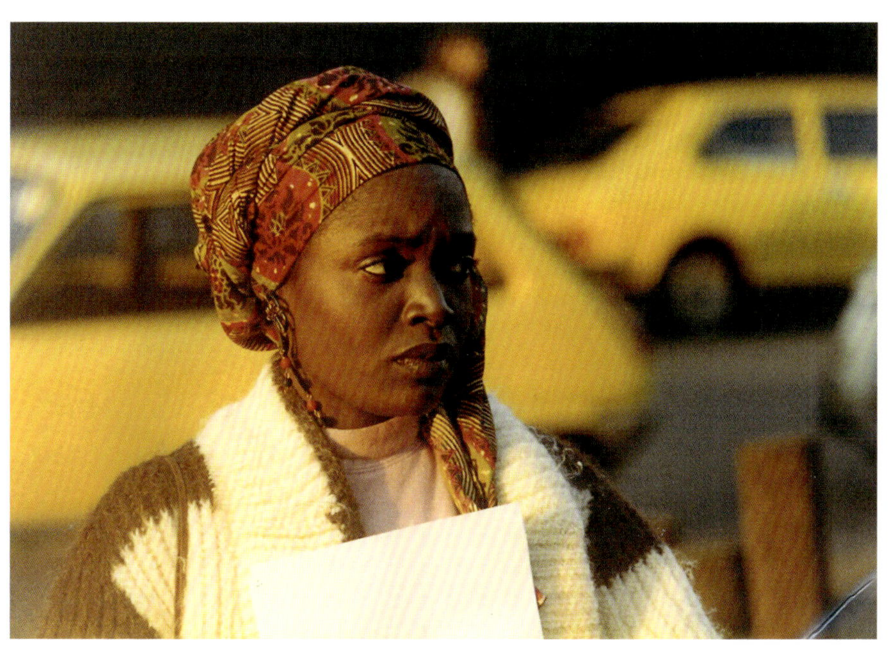

Tam Joseph b.1947

The painted triptych, *UK School Report* reads 'Good at Sports, Likes music, Needs surveillance'; it is amusing and then uncomfortable. Dominican-born Tam Joseph depicts a Black male in his key developmental stages: as a child, a teenager and a young adult, his varying faces in red, white and blue. His natural hair springs over time, but his broad nose and full lips remain a constant. Joseph confirms this punctuation: 'Those who talked about identity were a nuisance. The moment the same youth – the athletic, the musical one – becomes assertive he becomes a problem. He becomes Black.'[17]

Today, such racial biases and school teachers' low expectations continue to affect the assessment outcomes of Black students in Britain, and the disciplinary measures taken against them. Enforced racial stereotypes, low attainment and a less than culturally competent curriculum has meant that more than sixty years after Joseph created his painting, Black pupils still obtain fewer qualifications than their peers and are excluded from school more often.

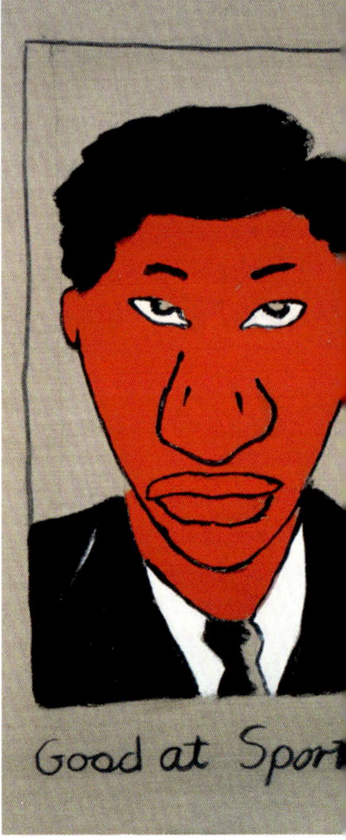

UK School Report 1983
Acrylic paint on canvas
85 x 120

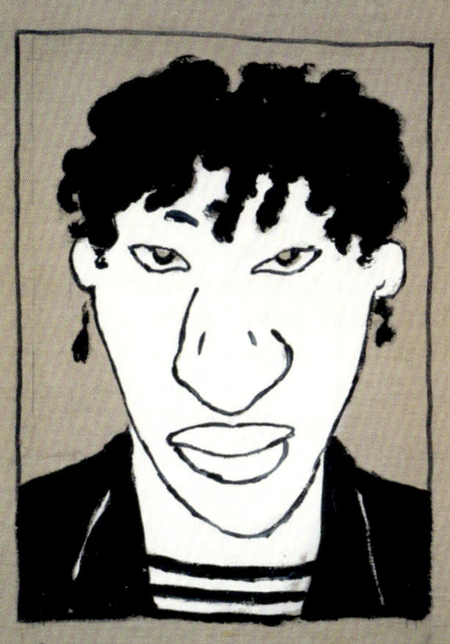

likes music

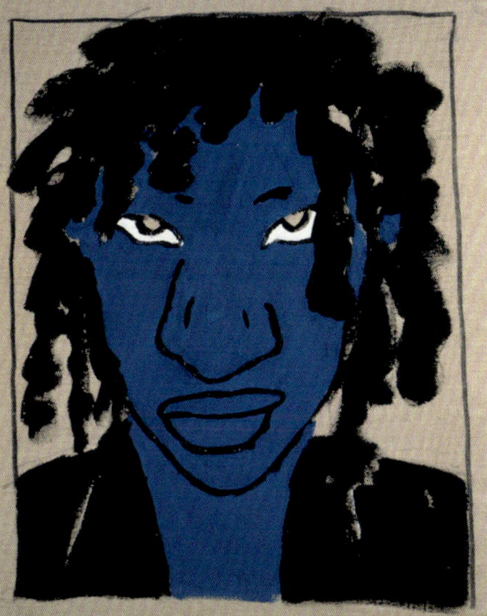

Needs surveillance

Bill Ming b.1944

Painter and sculptor Bill Ming says of himself: 'Like many African artists I am a wood carver and storyteller, sharing my visions and messages with a multicultural village that links instinct with a contemporary perspective through my education and experience. These ideas are reflected in my sculpture as well as collage. I often reuse old work along with fragments of timber and found objects. They exist as a kind of cultural archaeology, their present meanings both echoing and reflected in time gone by.'[18]

After working as a cook on the ocean liners that ferried people between the US, UK and the Caribbean, Ming left Bermuda for the UK in 1971, at the age of twenty-eight. With minimal qualifications he had to begin education at the level of a fourteen-year-old and experience being the only Black man in the school.

In *A Lesson in Trust*, Ming inserted a representative figure of himself as a role model willing to openly embrace his fellow man. In the artist's own words:

'This sculpture aims to portray positive interaction, understanding and support for one another.

Whether Father/Mother
Sister or Brother
we gotta love one/n/other
that's a must

We all need A Lesson in Trust.' [19]

A Lesson in Trust 1984
Limewood
72 x 66 x 27

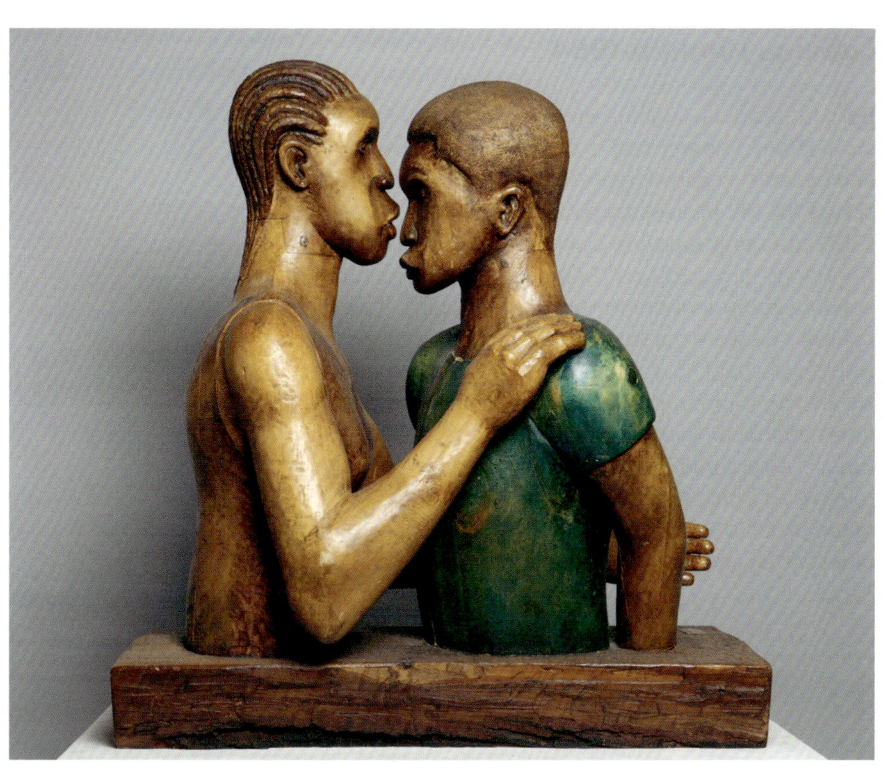

Lubaina Himid b.1954

Born in Tanzania, Lubaina Himid relocated to England as an infant. She went on to co-found the Blk Art Group and became a central figure in Black women's groups across the UK. In an essay published in Maud Sulter's 1990 anthology *Passion: Discourses on Blackwomen's Creativity,* Himid affirms: 'Being the first has its triumphs, keeping going is where the hard work begins. If we really believed we were the first Black women to call ourselves artists we would have an excuse to give up, we were not, we are the continuum. We are part of an enormous international movement which stretches far back in time.'[20] After three decades of pivoting between major roles as an artist, curator, critic, archivist and educator of the Black Arts movement, in 2017 Himid became the oldest artist and first Black woman to win the prestigious Turner Prize.

Freedom and Change is an historical revision of Picasso's 1922 painting *Two Women Running on the Beach (The Race).* In Himid's version, a large-scale pink bedsheet is used as a canvas and is hung by clothespins. Two Black women clothed in mosaic patterns are holding hands with their bald heads flung back. They are being pulled along by four snarling guard dogs on leashes. Behind them are the plywood heads of white men. In this appropriation, the two women, who are personifications of freedom and change, look daringly to the future while disregarding the static past.

Freedom and Change 1984
Wood, textiles, cardboard, paint, graphite, coloured pencil, chalk and ink
309.6 x 590 x 6

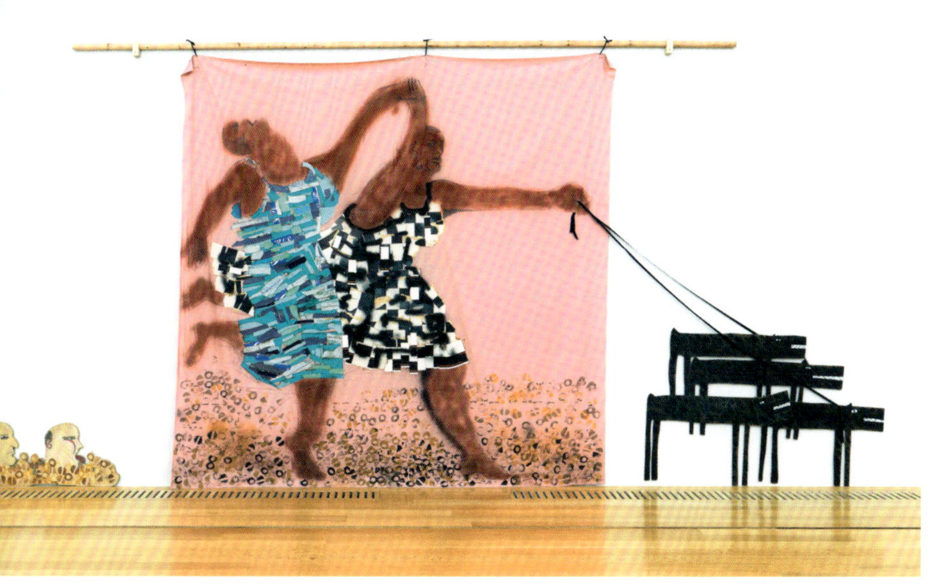

Pogus Caesar b.1953

The photographer who freeze-framed the 'Black bomber'
that appeared on the front page of every national tabloid
newspaper in September 1985, days after the Handsworth
uprisings in Birmingham, remains unknown, but the more
ambiguous image of a Molotov cocktail held in a Black fist
was captured on a Cannon Auto Focus 35mm, by Pogus
Caesar, who was mindful not to implicate any of the
protestors. Caesar explains: 'Those riots were the result
of frustration built up over years of people suffering from
poor job prospects, poor housing, poverty, harassment,
racism, and a "them-and-us" situation. I can remember
the smells and the sounds, there was fear and excitement
and danger. This was a scene of devastation and anger,
people running backward and forwards.'[21]

Caesar would inspect the *National Geographic* and
Readers' Digest which granted him access to photography
as a pre-teen West Indian living in England. In an
interview, he said : 'In the early 1980s, I purchased a
35mm film camera, a Canon AF, which is still in use today.
The fact that I only had 36 frames at my disposal taught
me about patience and economy.'[22]

Exhibiting his work often, Caesar represented his home
island of St Kitts in the *Caribbean Expressions in Britain*
exhibition (1986)[23] and was also included in the Black Art
Gallery's debut show *Heart in Exile* (1983).[24]

Petrol bomb in Handsworth
1985
Gelatin silver print on
paper 25 x 35

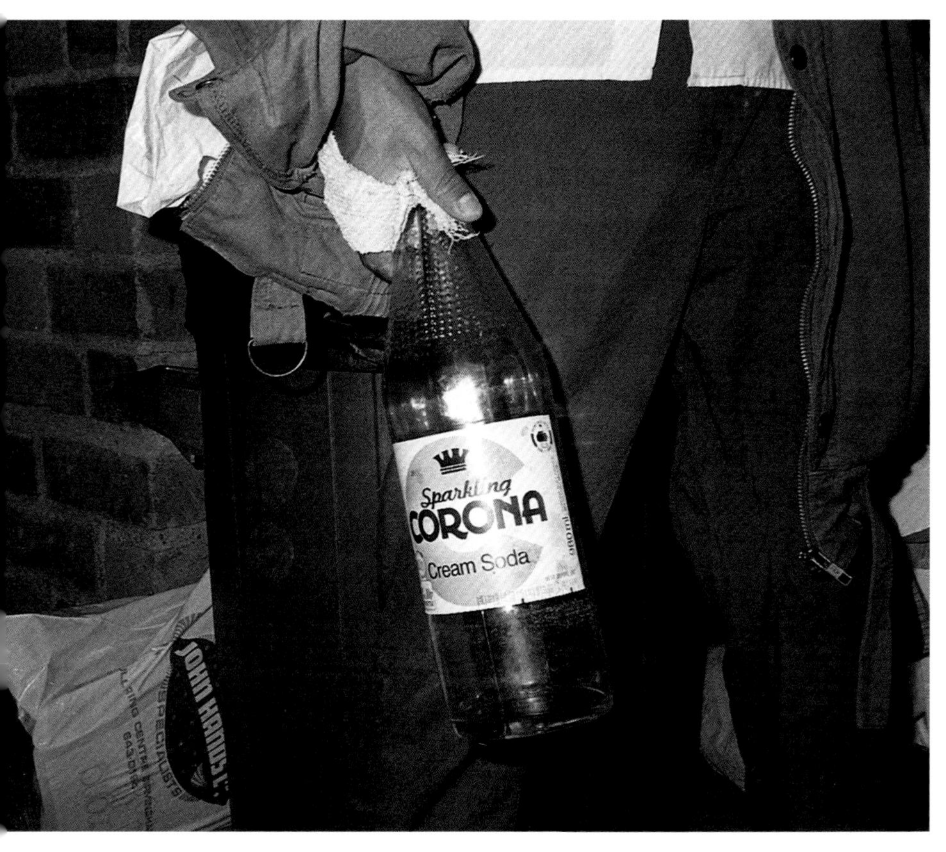

Sparkling
CORONA
Cream Soda

Ceddo Film and Video Workshop

Named after a 1977 film by Senegalese film director Ousmane Sembène, Ceddo translates loosely as 'the resistance of a culture'. The original members of Ceddo Film and Video Workshop – Milton Bryan, Imruh Bakari Caesar, Roy Cornwall, Dada Imarogbe, Glenn Ujebe Masokoane, June Reid and Menelik Shabazz, later joined by more female members such as D. Elmina Davis and Valerie Thomas, and then others – distinguished themselves from other collectives in their commitment to portraying African and Caribbean lives in Britain. From 1982 to 1989, Ceddo's members produced documentaries about the struggle against South-African apartheid, Rastafari women and sickle-cell anaemia.[25]

The collective's first film for Channel 4, *The People's Account,* was a documentary about the Broadwater Farm uprising in Tottenham, London, commissioned in part in response to earlier social unrest. The film opens to the score of the reggae group Black Uhuru and this narration: 'Three major uprisings rocked London and Birmingham in late 1985. Each was sparked by an act of police lawlessness against a Black woman.' The Ceddo members refused to cede to censorship, and so Channel 4 declined to air *The People's Account* and it was never shown on British television.

The People's Account 1985
Film; colour and sound
50 min

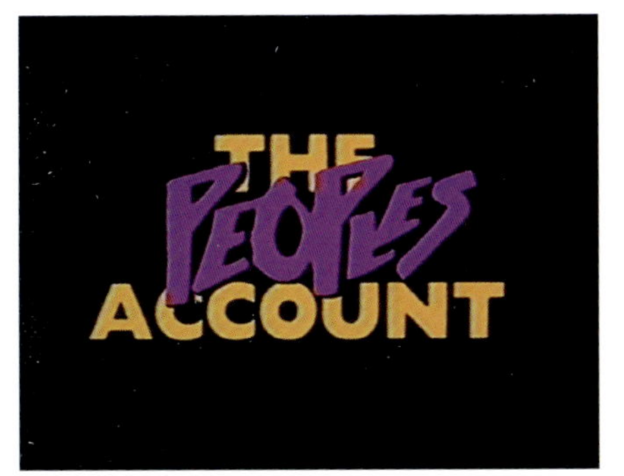

THE
PEOPLES
ACCOUNT

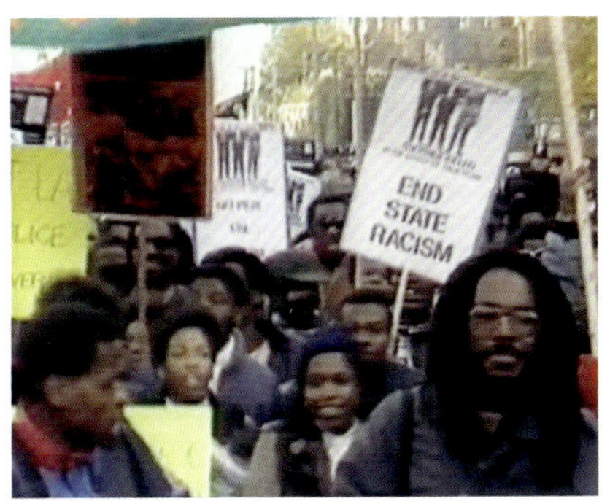

END
STATE
RACISM

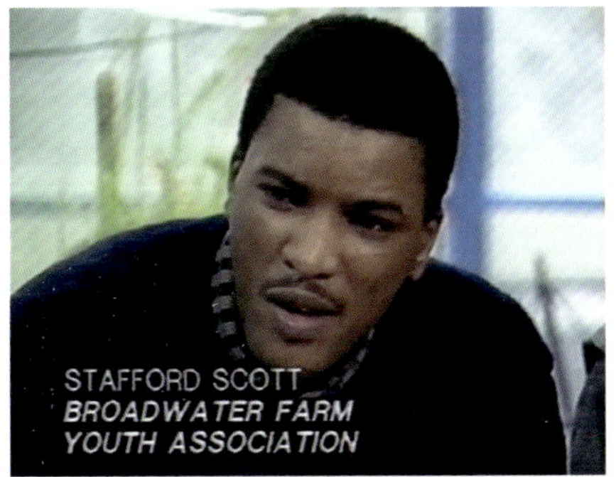

STAFFORD SCOTT
BROADWATER FARM
YOUTH ASSOCIATION

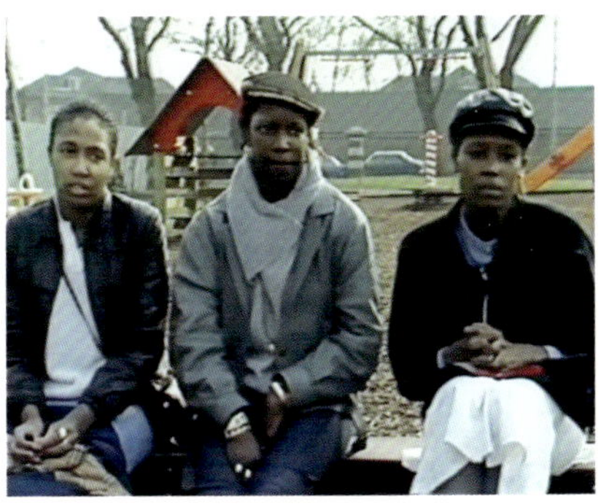

Sonia Boyce b.1962

Sonia Boyce was born in London to Bajan and Guyanese parents. Her work is marked by three phases: in the 1980s, crediting the influence of Frida Kahlo (1907–54), she produced some of her best known large-scale pastel drawings. Boyce then turned her attention to figurative representations of Black women (including herself) such as: *Big Woman Talk* 1984, *Auntie Enid, The Pose* (illustrated here) and *She Ain't Holding Them up, She's Holding on (Some English Rose)* 1986. She would later move into collage and installation.

A key member of the Blk Art Group, Boyce's investment in the representation of Black art has continued over the decades. A long overdue acknowledgment on a grand scale finally came for Boyce: in 2022 she will be the first Black woman to represent Great Britain at the prestigious Venice Biennale.

Auntie Enid, The Pose 1985
Pastel and oil pastel on
paper 183 x 122

With *Auntie Enid, The Pose* the artist immortalises her aunt, well-dressed and primped, in a life-size canvas using pastel and oil pastels. The work references the 1960s black-and-white studio portraits that were common to Caribbean immigrants at the time, and which were used to document their existence and progress in Britain. Interior details – a dark carpet, patterned wallpaper and decorative table – are new additions to reflect a domestic West Indian aesthetic.

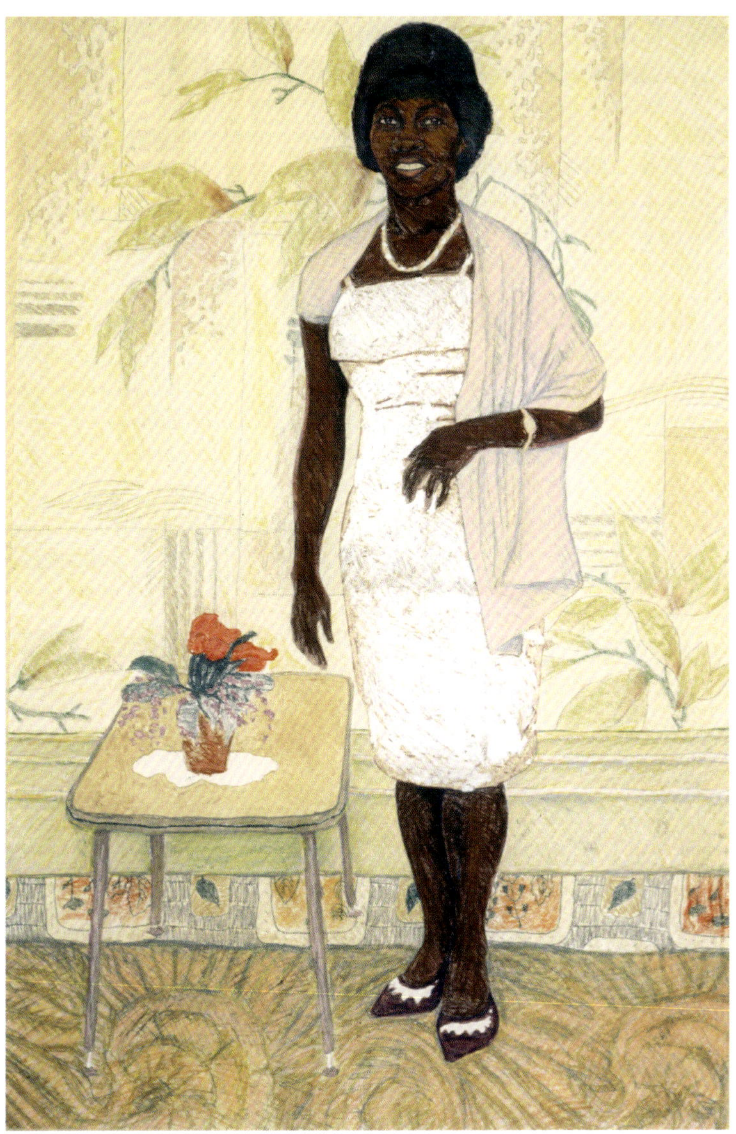

Black Audio Film Collective

Black Audio Film Collective's manifesto states: 'Our point of entry is around the issue of Black representation. The Collective was launched with three principal aims. Firstly, to attempt to look critically at how racist ideas and images of Black people are structured and presented as self-evident truths in cinema. What we are interested in here is how these "self-evident truths" become the conventional pattern through which the Black presence in cinema is secured.'[26]

Handsworth Songs is a film essay comprised of originally-shot documentary film footage, still photographs, tableau vivants, and newsreel footage from the 1960s and the 1985 riots in the UK. These disturbances flared up primarily in response to the consistent lethal policing of Black British communities in 1980s Britain. The film was awarded several international awards, including the Grierson Award for Best Documentary.

Handsworth Songs 1986
Film; single-channel
16 mm, colour and sound
58 min, 33 sec

Black Audio Film Collective's members were John Akomfrah, Reece Auguiste, Lina Gopaul, Avril Johnson, Edward George, David Lawson and Trevor Mathison. Over a sixteen-year span, Black Audio Film Collective presented an avant-garde filmmaking practice that saw its work exhibited on mainstream television, at A-List international film festivals and international art galleries, as well as at local community centres.

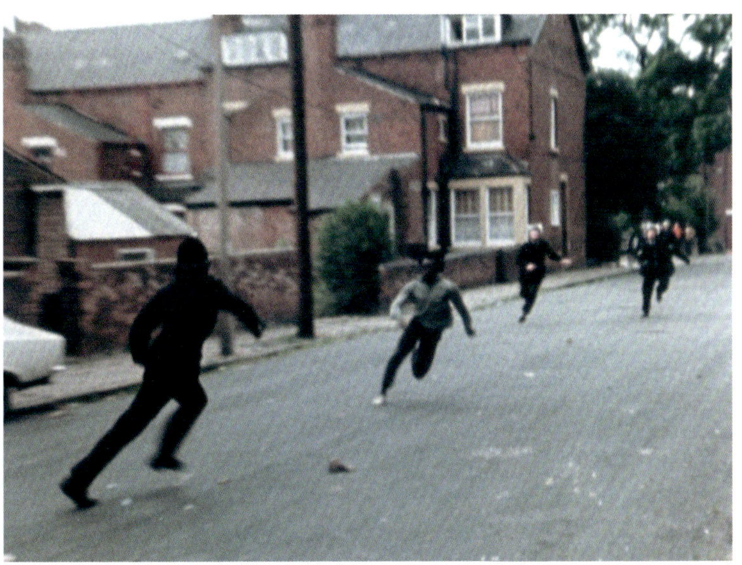

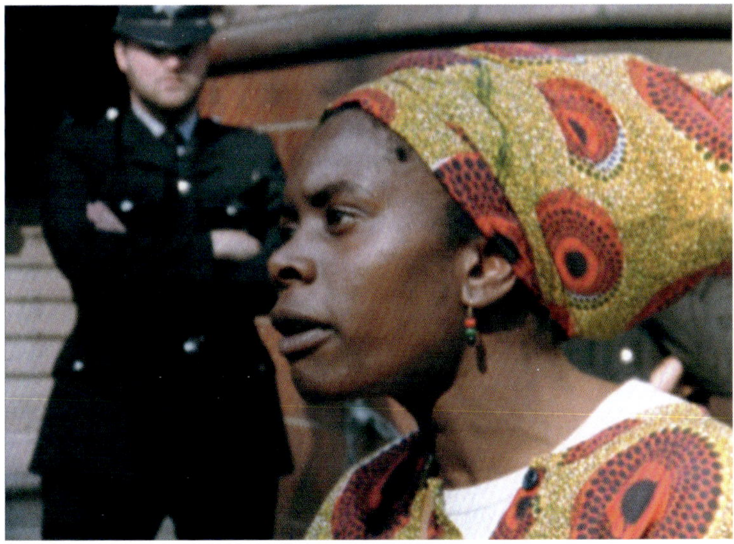

Sankofa Film Collective

Martina Attille, Maureen Blackwood, Nadine Marsh-Edwards and Isaac Julien made up the Sankofa Film Collective. Their first film, produced by the collective but directed by Julien, *Who Killed Colin Roach?* 1983, was concerned with the death of a young Black British man in the foyer of Stoke Newington police station. Subsequently, *Territories* looks at the Notting Hill Carnival riots in 1976, where resistance to arbitrary police arrests and harassment erupted into hours of unrest and damaged property.

The director of these films, Isaac Julien, shared the motivation behind them in an interview with the artist, writer and curator Coco Fusco in 1988: 'Questions of the diaspora, questions of policing. The significance of the sound systems in the carnival. In other words, what does Blackness mean to a Black culture? That was the main question. (…) I can look back on it now and I can see how I was trying to break with the realist debate and do something else. I can see now how the format I chose also had its limitations, but it was important for me at the time to try to do something like that. I saw *Territories* as a film essay around civil disorder and semiological questions for Black people.'[27]

Territories 1984
Film; 16mm; shown as
video, projection, colour
and sound
25 min, 45 sec

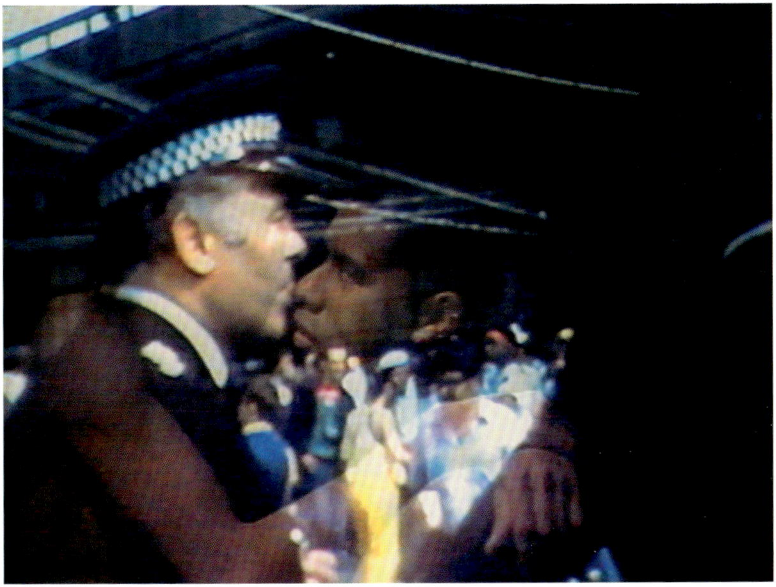

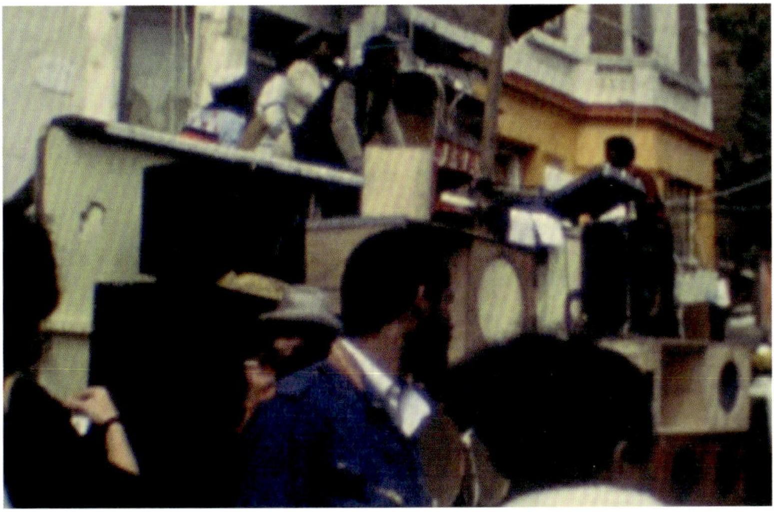

Marlene Smith b.1964

Artist and curator Marlene Smith's homonymous and unassuming mixed-media work *Art History* is one of high sentimentality and kitsch. Bright, artificial flowers sit inside a crochet-covered vase which rests on a white plinth next to four small images hung vertically in clip-frames. In this piece overlooked Black women and their creativity are strategically staged: nineteenth-century Black American sculptor Edmonia Lewis is represented in a photocopied image; the artist Simonè Alexander's self-portrait is made in oil paint; the hands of potter Magdalene Odundo appear in a photograph taken by Ingrid Pollard, along with *Portrait of Our Time* by photographer Brenda Agard. The crocheted vase was made by the artist's mother, who stiffened it with sugar-water. The simplicity does not weaken the aesthetic and political value.

Smith was a member of the Blk Art Group, and joined the group after seeing *The Pan Afrikan Connection: An Exhibition by Young Black British Artists* at Ikon Gallery in her hometown Birmingham, organised by the collective in 1982. Later she would undertake an apprenticeship at the Black-Art Gallery in north London, eventually taking on the role of director.

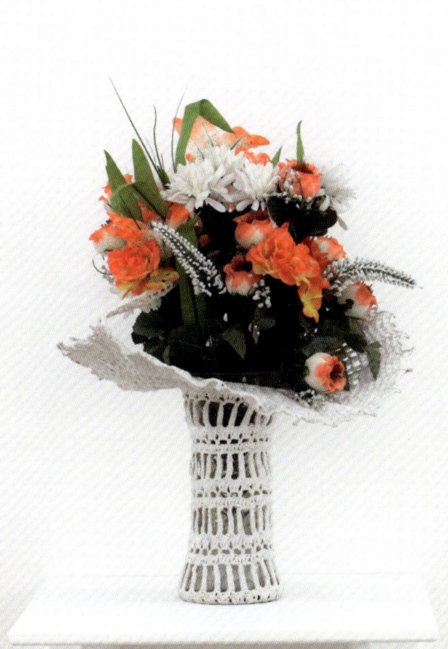

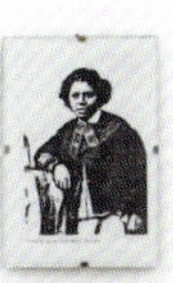

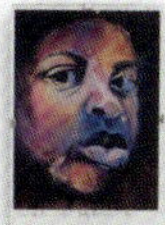

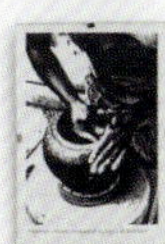

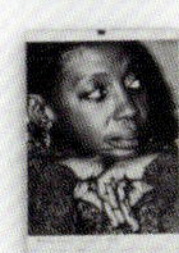

Keith Piper b.1960

Go West Young Man is a series of fourteen black-and-white panels of photomontage and handwritten text. With it, mixed-media artist Keith Piper repurposes the disturbingly violent and graphic plan of an English slave ship, 'The Brookes', that was originally published by the Plymouth Chapter of the 'Society for Effecting the Abolition of the Slave Trade' in 1788. Scribed underneath is the 1865 call by newspaper editor Horace Greeley, for white men to settle in America. *Go West Young Man* would later be adapted into a short film in 1996.

The founding member of the Blk Art Group was born in Malta due to his father's deployment in the RAF, but he was raised by his Montserratian and Antiguan parents in Birmingham. Reflecting on his most referenced artwork, Piper notes: 'I first juxtaposed these two signs within an artwork in the late 1970s whilst still at school with little knowledge of the specific provenance of either the image or the text. I was however struck by the ironic tension generated between this optimistic invocation to embrace the "west" and all that it offered, and the harsh realities of the forced transportation of African peoples into the Western hemisphere via the terrors of the "middle passage".'[28]

Go West Young Man 1987
1 of 14 photographs; gelatin silver prints on paper mounted onto board
84 × 56

Go West

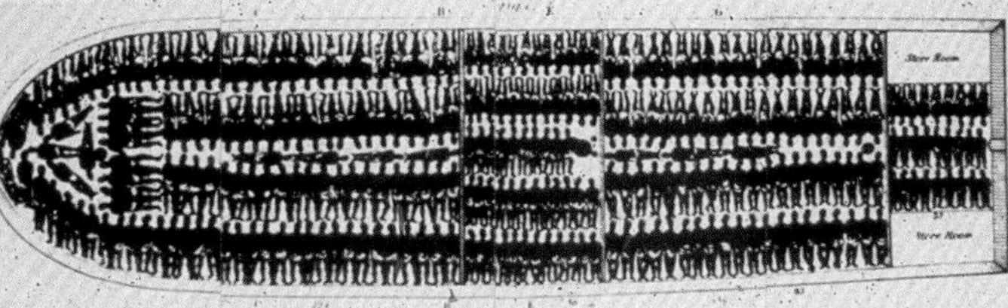

YOUNG MAN

Rotimi Fani-Kayode 1955–89

Born in Nigeria, Rotimi Fani-Kayode presented as Black and gay in the 1980s, when he lived in London with his lover and collaborator, Alex Hirst. Having experienced the kind of contentiousness that greeted Black artists in the UK, Fani-Kayode once wrote about 'Europeans faced with the dogged survival of alien cultures' and their tendency to act 'as mercantile as they were in the days of the Trade.' Such observers, he continued with disdain, are on a mission to 'sell our culture as a consumer product.'[29]

In his 2019 book *Decolonising the Camera: Photography in Racial Time,* British curator Mark Sealy employs his concept of 'racial time' to 'signify a different but essential colonial temporality at work within a photograph'[30] – an idea that applies to images by Fani-Kayode. His studio-based photography, much of it self-portraiture, is of a theatrical, sensual and serious nature – and it plays with conventions and expectations, too: In *Untitled (Offering),* the conception of the hyper-eroticised Black phallus is represented by a pair of overly large scissors.

Untitled (Offering) c.1987
Gelatin silver print on
paper 50.8 x 61

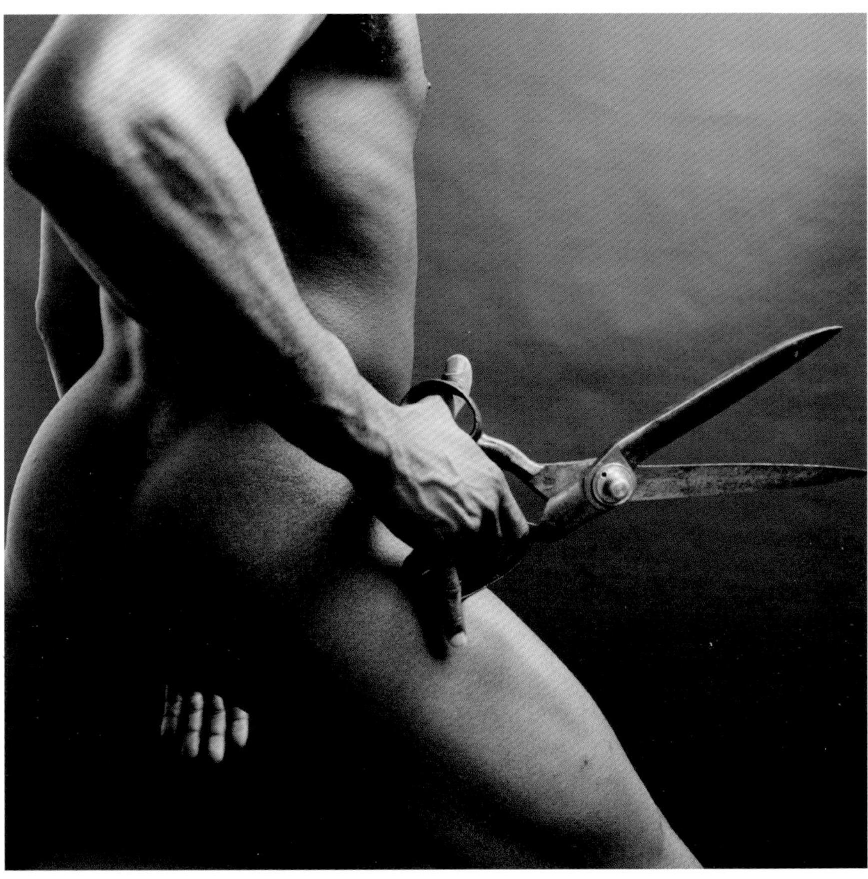

Norman 'Normski' Anderson b.1966

At the age of nine, Norman Anderson anticipated receiving a bicycle from his mother in hopes of cheering him up after a period of sickness. But with none left at the local auction, he settled for a Kodak 126 Instamatic camera for £3.

By the age of eighteen, Anderson was working as a freelance photographer for music and fashion magazines. He profiled some of London's earliest 1980s rap groups, such as She Rockers (illustrated here)[31], and The Demon Boys, as well as monumental cultural events such as the Def Jam tour of 1987 with LL Cool J, Eric B & Rakim and Public Enemy. He would continue to document the rise of Hip Hop throughout the 2000s. Anderson is reminiscent of that time: 'As I have lived in London all my life you'll see that my images are taken from a UK perspective and I hope show that none of the UK artists were pumped full of money, but rather they had an attitude and a hunger to prove they had a voice and a look that we could call our own.'[32]

She Rockers Shepherd's Bush Green 1988
35mm colour transparency film, printed on paper
68 x 57

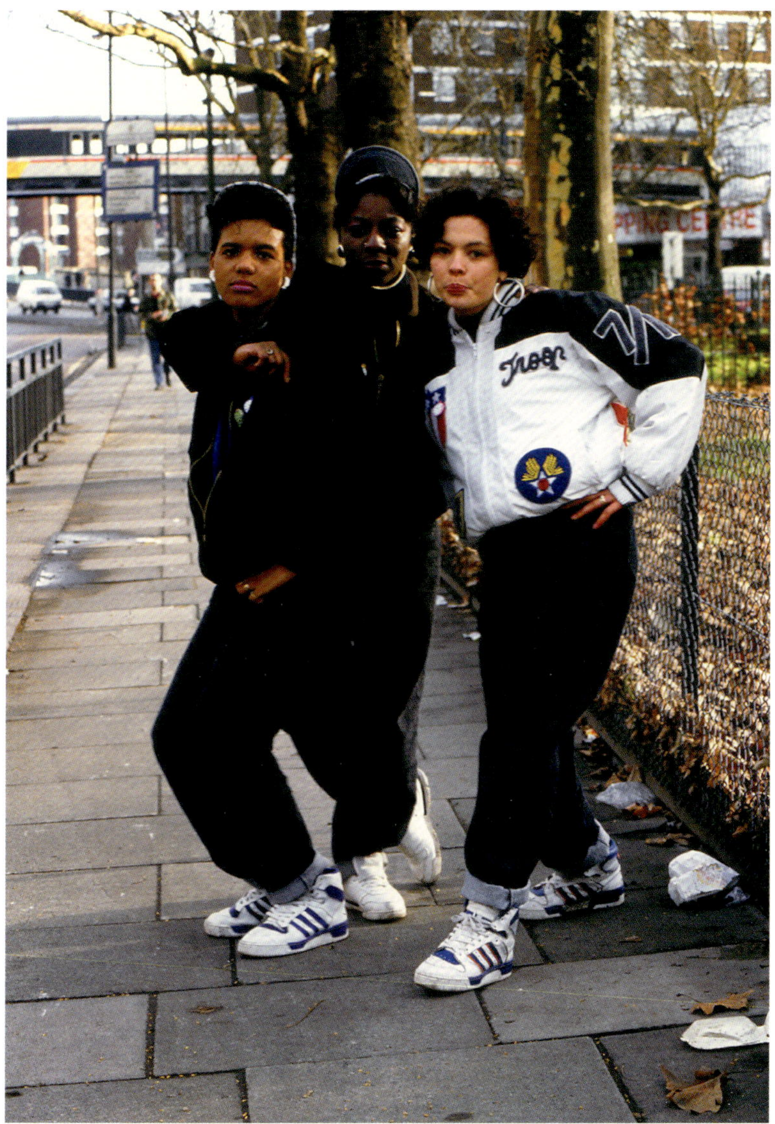

Ingrid Pollard b.1953

Ingrid Pollard arrived in England from Guyana, with her sister, at the age of four. Her parents, who arrived in the UK separately, brought with them family photo albums. She would later include some of this material in her work. Pollard has sustained her photographic practice since the late 1980s, and was a founding member of Autograph, the Association of Black British Photographers, as it was known until 2017.

In the series *Oceans Apart* a Black family is interacting in a British coastal setting in what is an almost unrecognisable scene compared to the more common visual representation of Black communities in major cities such as London and Birmingham. Commenting on the series, Pollard explains: 'The Atlantic Ocean as physical and psyche space forms the basis of this work. During the last 600 years, the coastal areas stretching from the eastern shores of the Caribbean to the Atlantic coast of America seem to have been connected to the western shores and England and Europe. These have been sites of important arrivals and departures.'[33]

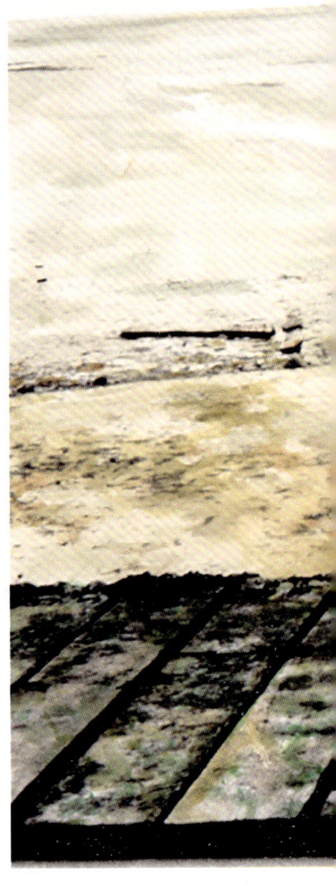

Oceans Apart 1989
1 of 11 hand-tinted gelatin
silver prints on paper
with text 52.5 x 62.8

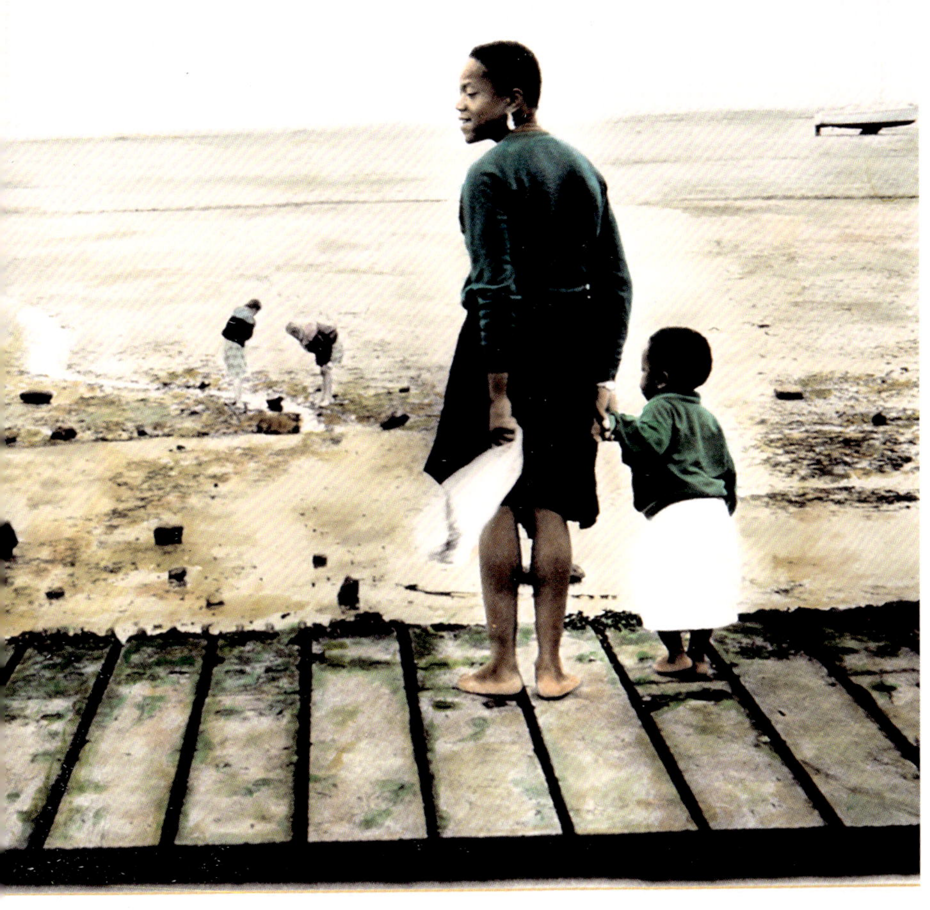

Amani Napthali b.1962

The parodic stage play *Ragamuffin* (1989) politically
and socially binds the 1985 Broadwater Farm uprising
in Tottenham, in response to a police-killing of Cynthia
Garrett, to the Saint-Domingue revolution that made
Haiti the first Black republic in the Western hemisphere.
The Supreme Court of African Justice set is marked by
a DJ booth on top of a housing estate and colourful artist
depictions of Marcus Garvey, Toussaint L'Ouverture
and Emperor Haile Selassie.

On trial is the allegorical boasy and politically disillusioned
Black man called Ragamuffin, who is simultaneously
blamed and praised for the revolting. The call and
response musical sets the visceral mood spreading
throughout Black Britain at the time. The play is
authentically reflective of the times when Black Britons
felt some of the first and deepest effects of Thatcherism
through labour exploitation, the racist criminalisation
of Black culture and political exclusion.

London-born to Jamaican parents, Amani Napthali is
a dramatist and director trained in community theatre
arts and film and television production, and is a founding
member of the Double Edge Theatre Company formed
in 1984. Napthali considers his practice, made up of
countless productions, to be 'ritualistic art'. Of his
most-cited work he asserted that, 'Ragamuffin is a
seminal moment within the history of Black British theatre
and stands as a fitting testament to the ongoing strides,
struggles and artistic achievements made by the Black
Bohemians and other members of the Afrocentric
Avant-garde, for the establishment and evolution of a
truly African aesthetic within the UK creative industries.'[34]

Poster advertising
Ragamuffin at Library
Theatre, Manchester 1990
Printed ink on paper
59.4 x 42.1

DOUBLE EDGE THEATRE COMPANY LTD PRESENTS
RAGAMUFFIN

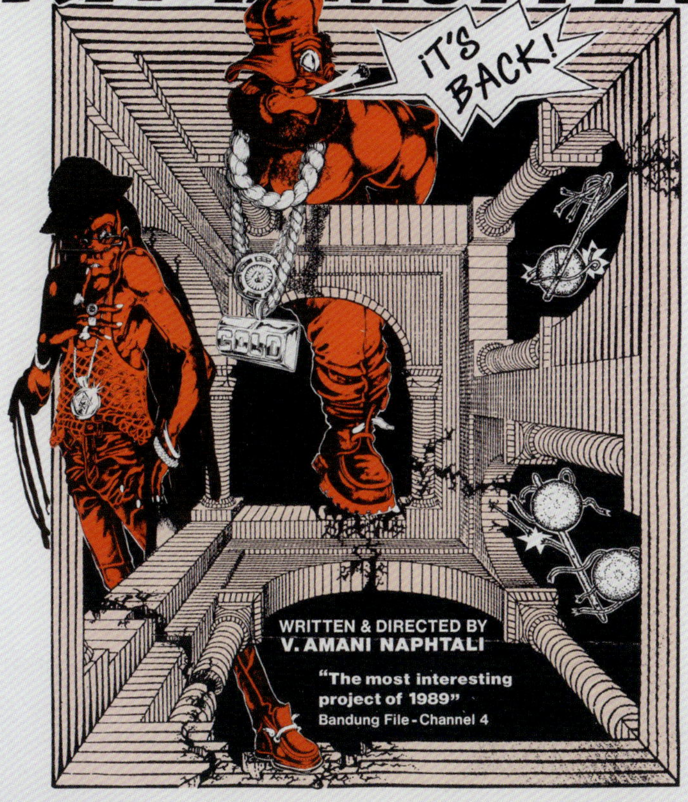

WRITTEN & DIRECTED BY
V. AMANI NAPHTALI

"The most interesting project of 1989"
Bandung File - Channel 4

THURS 20 SEPTEMBER – SAT 22 SEPTEMBER
7.30pm
St. Peters Square, Manchester M2.

Visa & Access
TEL: 061 236 7110

LIBRARY Theatre
MANCHESTER

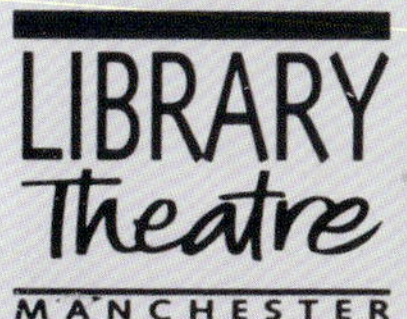

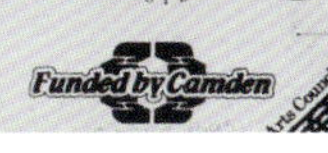

Joy Gregory b.1959

Raised in Buckinghamshire to Jamaican parents, Joy Gregory, like many of her artistic peers who were born in Britain, relied on a spectrum of mediums available to her in order to understand and express a national identity still new to most Black people. Though Gregory did not feel embraced by the mainstream Black Arts Movement, her particular expression of British Blackness eventually found its own place and audience.

Autoportrait consists of nine individual self-portraits that are arranged sequentially and presented as one. The black-and-white photographs are sharply contrasted; the slow development process is what gives the prints their distinct tone. In some frames, Joy Gregory's face is in full view, and in others the features of her face considered to be racial markers – full lips and kinky natural hair – are shown in close-up. Released in 1990, Gregory's unprecedented series was Autograph ABP's first artist commission and a counterpoise to the absence of Black women in beauty and style magazines. Gregory's concern with the constructions of beauty would continue to fuel the artist throughout her career, and would manifest in her work through a variety of photographic techniques, including Victorian printing.

Autoportrait 1989–90
9 portraits; gelatin silver prints on paper
60.96 x 50.8 each

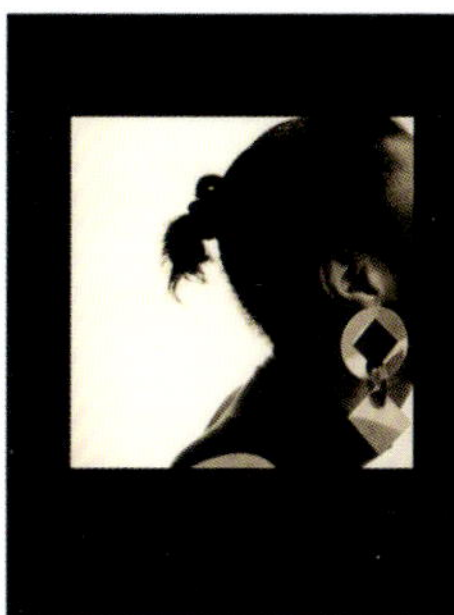
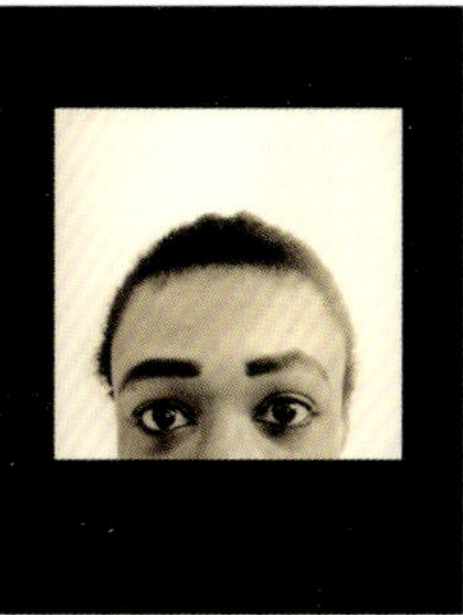
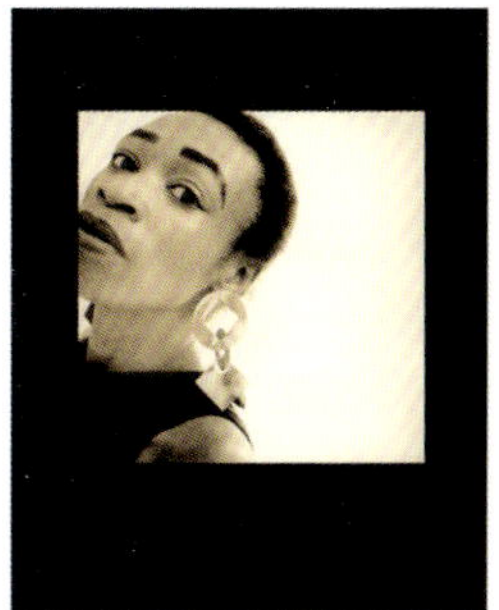
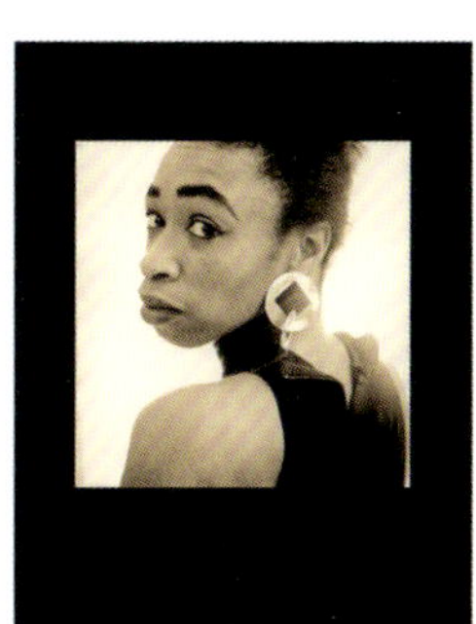
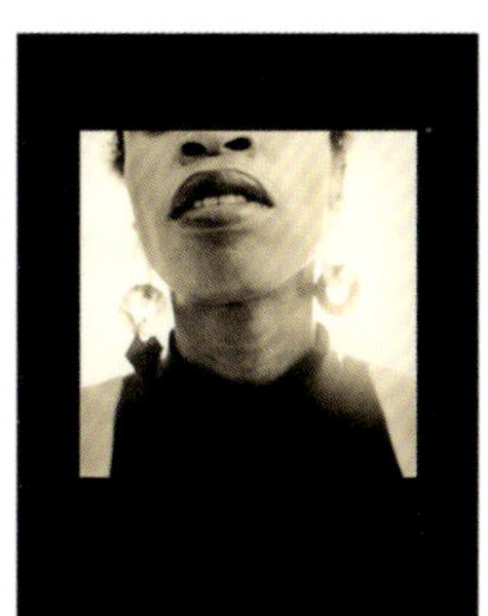
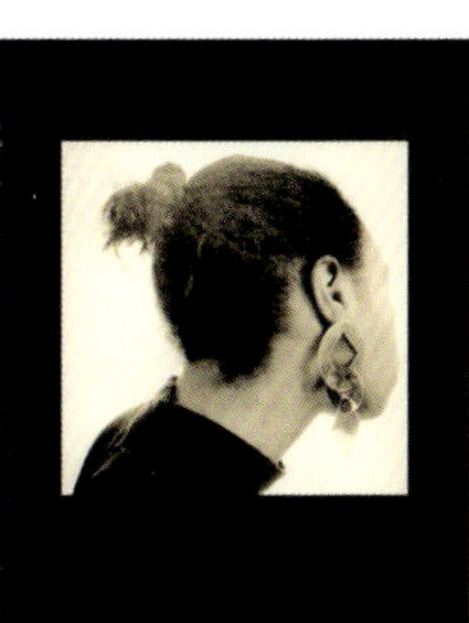
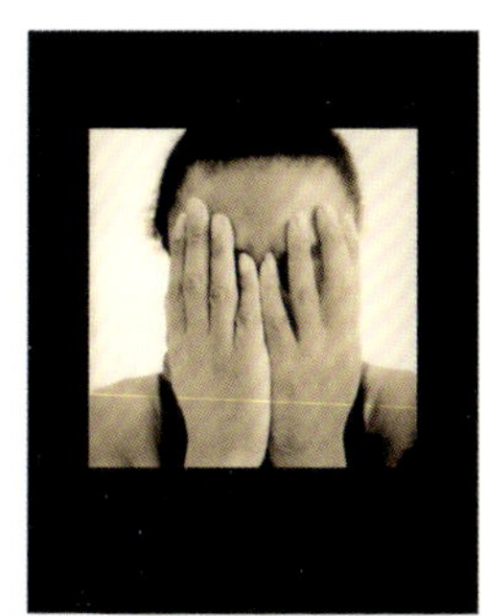
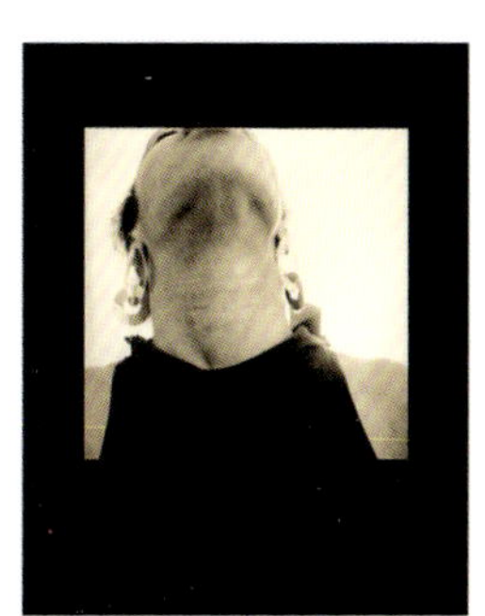
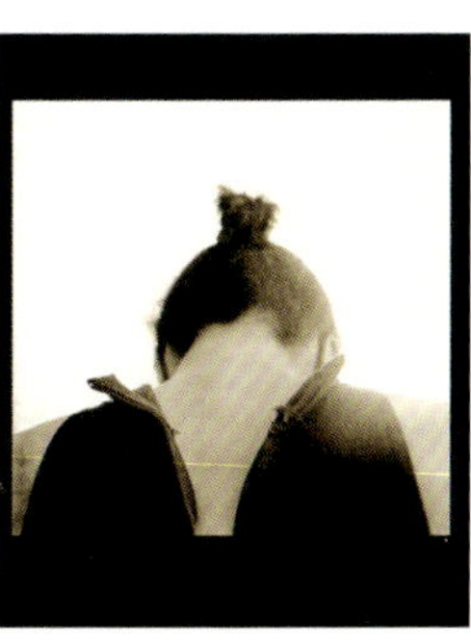

John Lyons b.1933

Painter and accomplished poet John Lyons came to England in the early 1960s and studied at Goldsmiths College in London, but it was as a young boy in Trinidad and Tobago, where he developed a deep affinity to drawing and sharing his art with his friends and neighbours.

Self-Portrait with Jumbie Bird and Alter Ego shows a human form where Trinidadian folklore rules and the famed devils, demons and other supernatural characters that appear in Trinidad's carnival take shape in bright oil paints. Lyons offers a comment: 'I can only say that there was an interesting and fun communication between this painting and my Trinidad and Tobago cultural self, if that makes any sense: The universal visual metaphor of the clown on the tightrope, representing my alter ego, with all that implies, is precariously balanced as a courageous act. The white owl (Jumbie bird) on my head has culturally numinous connotations; my balancing a paint brush on my finger tip suggests creative play with the same precariousness as the clown on the tightrope.'[35]

Self Portrait with Jumbie Bird and Alter Ego 1990
Oil paint on canvas
181.8 x 152.5

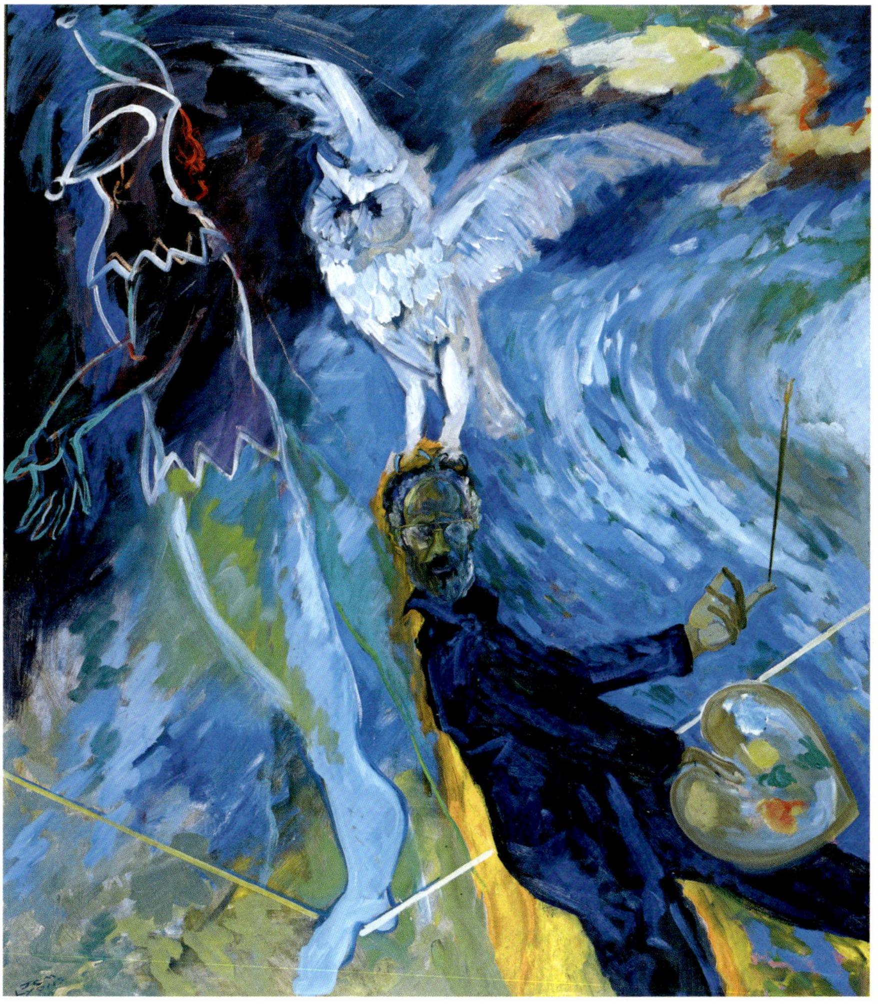

Donald Rodney 1961–98

In *Self-Portrait 'Black Men Public Enemy'*, Donald Rodney
returns to the topic of Black masculinity, considering
the positionality of himself and his peers in Britain –
essentially the social and political context that shapes
their identities and their respective views of the world.
Five portraits of Black men are displayed in lightboxes:
the first two are mugshots and the following two are of
a different man handcuffed. The identities of both men
are partially obscured by a black rectangle covering
their eyes. The final image is an 'identikit' composite
image commonly used in the media when searching
for suspected criminals. The Black man's selfhood is
irrevocably affected by false, negative and racist
representations of the Black man as an icon of danger.

Rodney, born in Birmingham to Jamaican parents, said
of the work: 'I wanted to make a self-portrait [though]
I didn't want to produce a picture with an image of myself
in it. It would be far too heroic considering the subject
matter. I wanted generic Black men, a group of faces that
represented in a stereotypical way [the] Black man as 'the
other', a Black man as the enemy within the body politic.'[36]

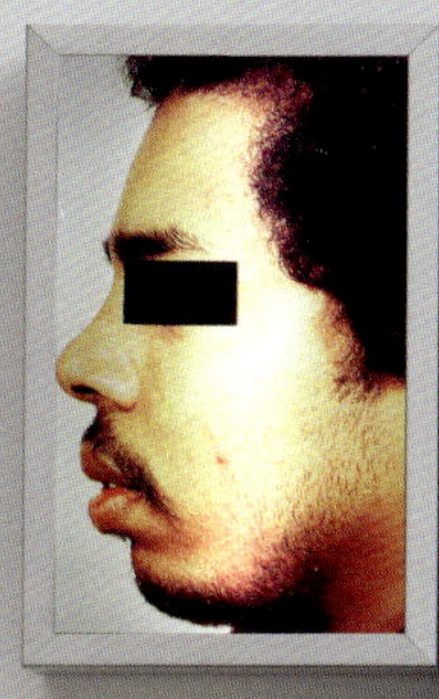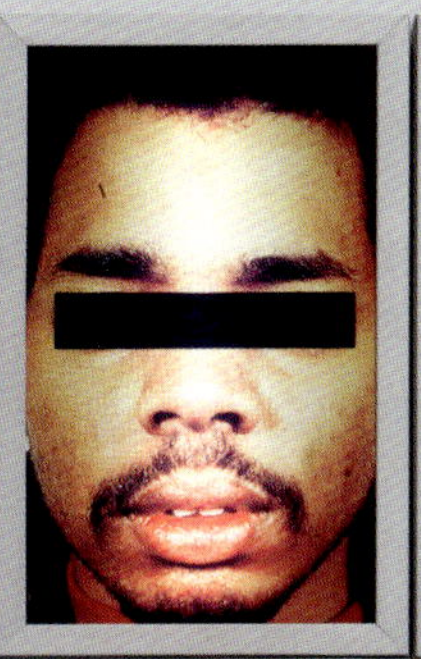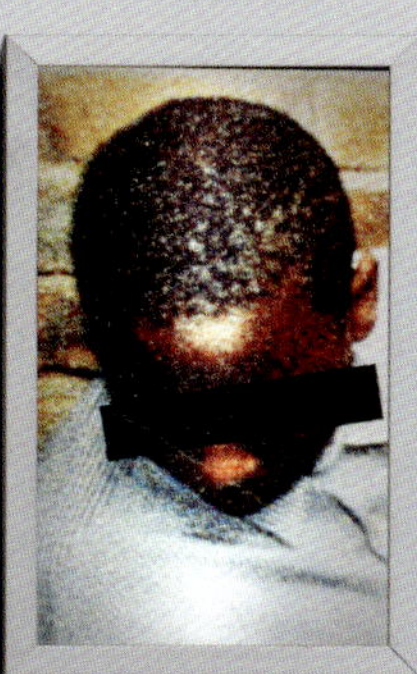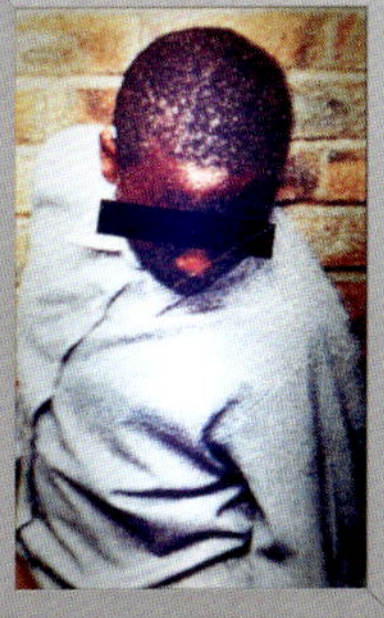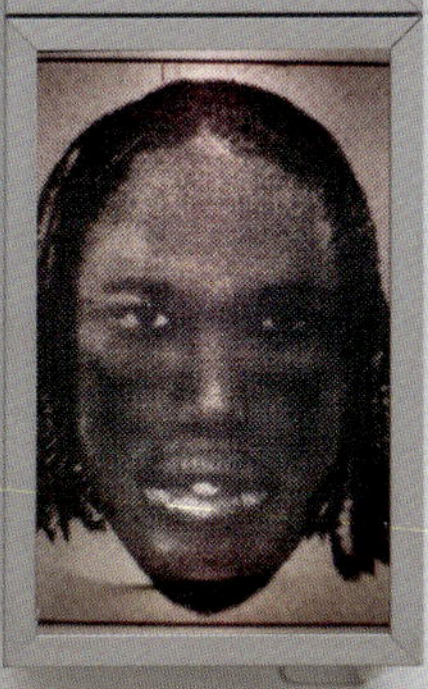

Isaac Julien b.1960

While still a student at Central Saint Martins, London, Isaac Julien co-founded Sankofa Film Collective (p.78) in 1983 and directed his first short *Who Killed Colin Roach?*. But it was his first feature-length film, *Young Soul Rebels,* which won the Semaine de la Critique prize for best film at the Cannes Film Festival in 1991. The drama-cum murder-mystery is set in the summer of 1977, the year of the Queen's Jubilee and the Battle of Lewisham – when the far-right National Front (NF) organised a march through multicultural areas of London – and follows two friends and music mavens: Caz, a Black homosexual, and Chris, a mixed-raced heterosexual, who run a pirate radio station specialising in soul music.

When asked by an American newspaper in the year of release about the representational work of his films, Julien responded: 'I deliberately wanted to work against "types" and obviously in the regime of representation of Black characters, they're always a "type." I'm interested in playing with people's expectations, especially in the context of talking about Black men. It's really difficult to contextualise gays in the same way.'[37]

Young Soul Rebels 1991
Film; colour and sound
105 min

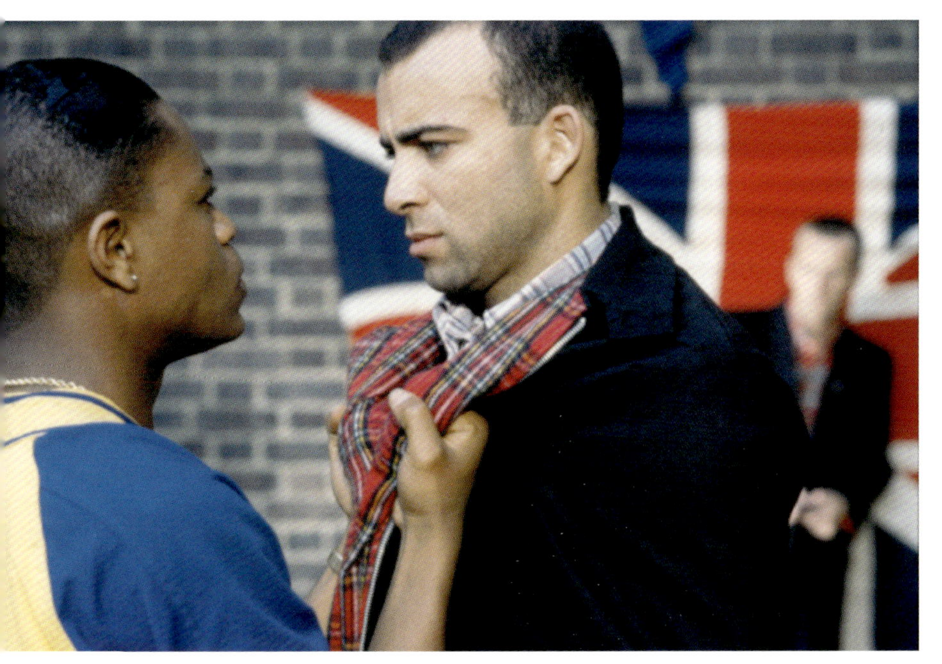

Maxine Walker b.1962

Despite only being active between 1985 and 1997, Birmingham-born Maxine Walker (of Jamaican parentage) co-founded the Monochrome Women's Photography Collective, Women + Photography, Polareyes and Autograph ABP. She was also an art critic, actively winning the support of her peers, Ingrid Pollard (p.88), Joy Gregory (p.92) and American artist Adrian Piper (b.1948). Responding to a question about visibility in an interview with Walker, Piper herself speculates: 'If I had stayed involved in the art world [in the] way that I was, my work would have been influenced by typical art world concerns instead of concerns having to do with my own identity as a Black woman.'[38]

In *Cleansing* Walker sits at a table in her bedroom, where the sanctified products of femininity – toner, eye gel, cotton wool, a vanity mirror – surround her on knitted doilies. With her hair wrapped in a white cloth and shoulders bare, Walker leans in to taste the rituals of womanhood, withdrawn but committed nonetheless.

The home is a contested site for Black women. Gendered and inherently political, it plays host to a sexist social history that defines domestic servitude as a woman's 'natural' role, along with child-rearing and pageantry. In spite of this, the home also serves as a place of refuge, rest, regeneration and meditation.

Cleansing 1991
From the series
Black Beauty 1991
Gelatin silver print on
paper 20.3 × 15.2

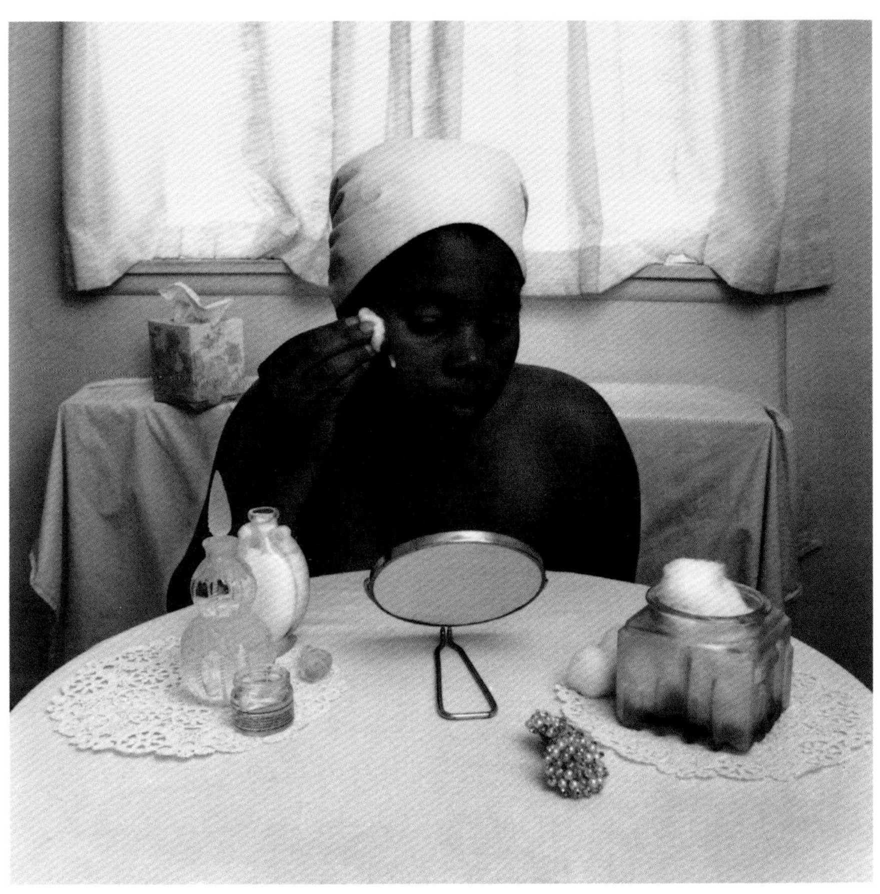

Steve McQueen b.1969

One of Steve McQueen's earliest films, *Exodus* is an adept example of the foundational centrality of the artist's hometown London to his artistic practice, despite having moved to Amsterdam in 1997. Born in London to Trinidadian and Grenadian parents, McQueen has asserted that his aspiration to be an artist was accomplished with 'hard-headedness and luck. Or hard-headedness and talent.'[39]

McQueen details why he instinctively began to follow the two middle-aged Black men wearing grey brimmed hats, neutral overcoats and carrying tall potted palms as they journeyed through the east London market: 'I was in Brick Lane market and I suddenly saw these palm trees walking towards me. I got out my camera and started shooting'. Twenty-two-year-old McQueen 'got the impression that they were in a relationship, that they were a couple', but the artist didn't insist on looking for evidence to 'prove it'.[40] The film is soundless; roused by the saturated colour of the Super 8 mm film, we watch the men bob and weave through crowds, as the plant stalks sway above their heads. They playfully dodge McQueen's view after their eyes catch the lens, but eventually the men board a red double-decker bus. They wave playfully from the top window at McQueen as the bus pulls away, and the brief sixty-five seconds of slow stealth action is looped.

Exodus 1992–7
Film; Super 8 mm,
shown as video, monitor,
colour (no sound)
1 min, 5 sec

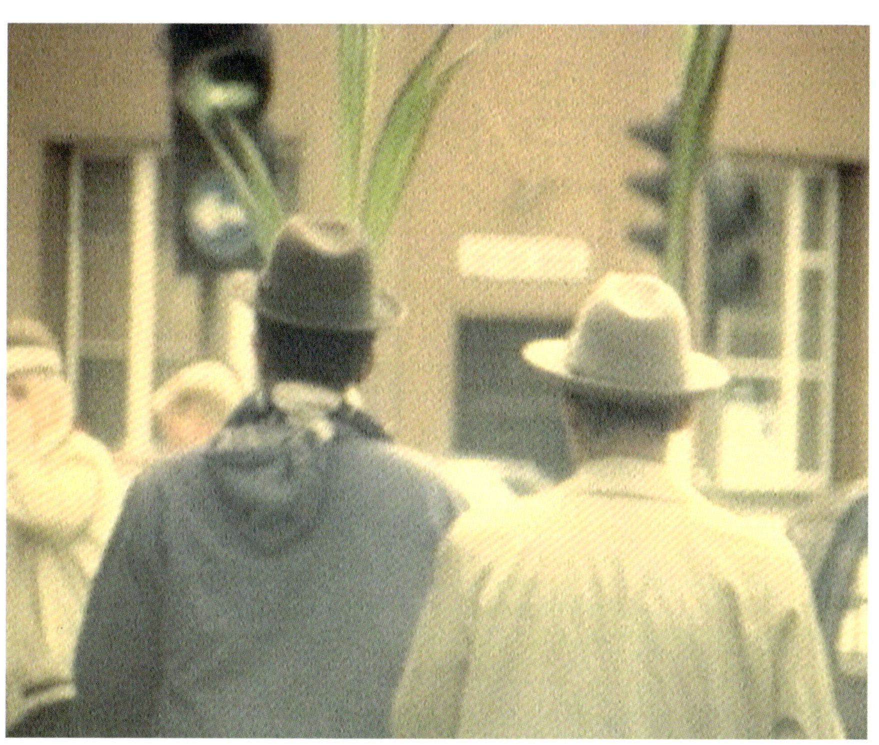

Ajamu b.1963

Huddersfield-born son of Jamaican parents Ajamu
adopted his African name from a mentor. In his early
twenties, after attending the first and only National Gay
Black Men's Conference in London in 1987, the artist cum
curator left northern England and its mostly invisible
queer Black community. Ajamu laments: 'Growing up in
the UK in the 1970s and early 80s, in mainstream popular
culture, all the images of gay men were white. Images of
Black men were always sports stars or in relation to
confrontations with authority. So for me there were very
few images I could relate to. So in a vague kind of way
I created images that just weren't there.'[41]

In *Heels* a pair of muscled calves stand as if to pirouette
in bedazzled heels, far from what is expected from the cis
Black male.

The 'rukus! Black, Lesbian, Gay, Bisexual and Trans
cultural archive, initiated by Ajamu and filmmaker Topher
Campbell in 2000, consists of diaries, letters, magazines,
flyers and photographs and is held in a public collection.

Heels 1993
Gelatin silver print on
paper 22 x 14

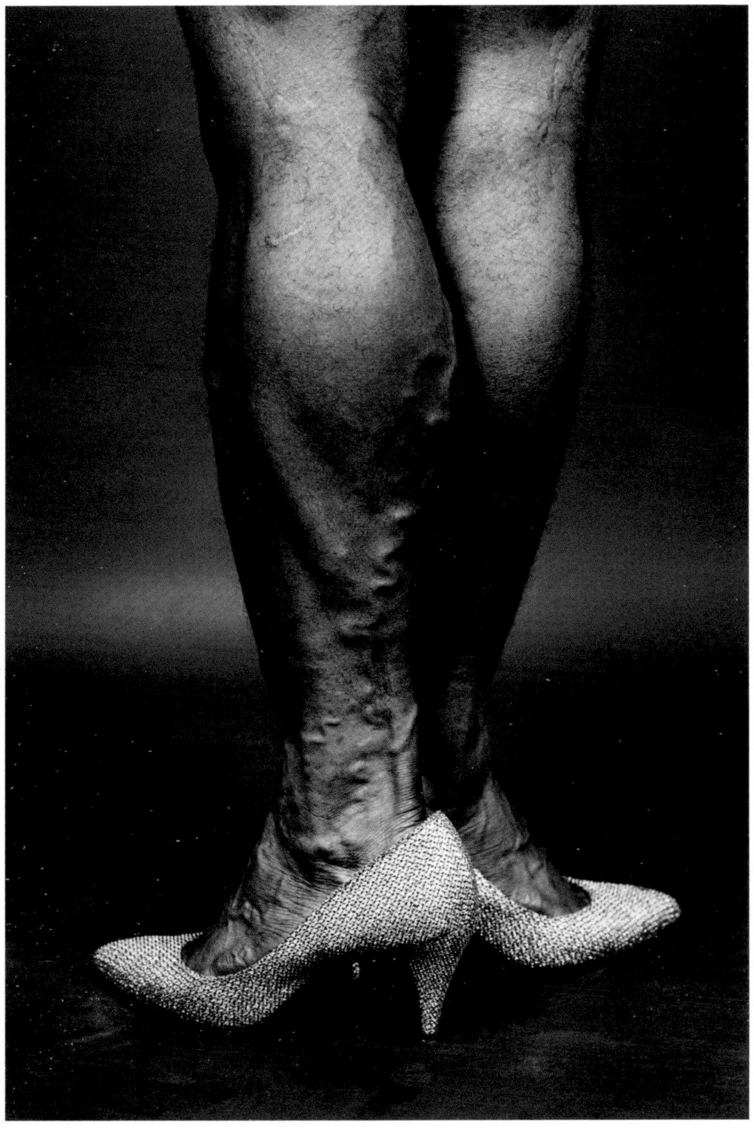

Jennie Baptiste b.1971

Originating in Jamaica, Reggae and eventually Dancehall held a firm place in Britain in the 1970s with its diaspora, but it was the 1990s sub-genre Ragga (often fused with Hip Hop) that rapidly gained traction with young Black people. At Dancehall events, elaborate styles of dancing, hair design, and bright and embellished clothes specially-made are the standard, as can be seen in Jenny Baptiste's *Ragga Crouching.* Today the performer in the photograph would be heralded as an immersive performance artist.

Originally dismissed by her college tutor as a 'throwaway culture', the Ragga project continued to drive Baptiste, who was London-born to St Lucian parents. Now, often in a teaching position herself, she notes: 'I have worked in photography and film with Black teens excluded from mainstream classes and the results of the work that they produce is astounding. I don't go into the classroom with a stereotypical vision of their capabilities because I have an understanding of how images can be created to focus on one dimension of someone's personality. You multiply that by a million times for a specific racial group and there you have a constructed stereotype.'[42]

Over the course of her career, Baptiste captured local and international musicians including Mary J. Blige, Nas and Roots Manuva, but *Ragga Crouching* remains one of the photographer's most widely seen images.

Ragga Crouching 1993
C-type print on paper
40.6 x 30.5

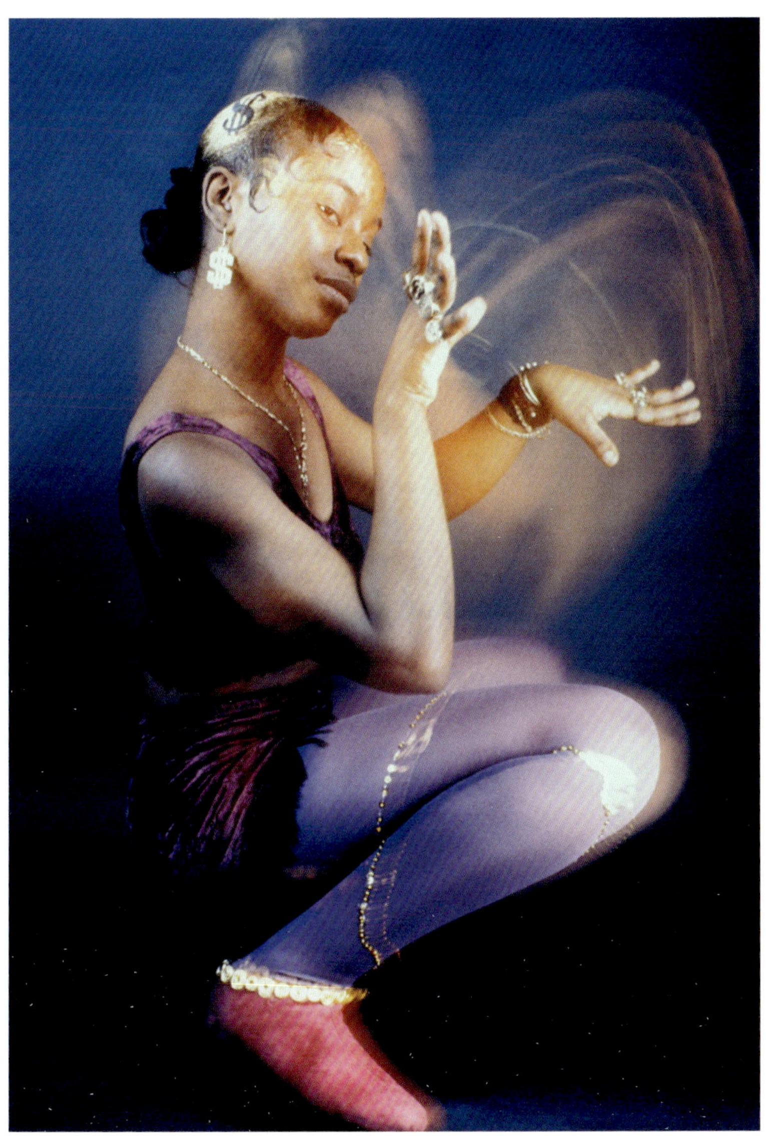

Emmanuel Taiwo Jegede b.1943

The painter and poet Emmanuel Taiwo Jegede trained as a sculptor in his local community, before advancing to the Yaba College of Technology in Lagos for decorating and painting. The formal elements of Jegede's Yoruba Ekiti heritage continue to appear in his image-making and poetry; his relocation to London and participation in the burgeoning 1980s Black British art scene did not distract from that.

The artist is known for his work with wood, bronze and ceramic; in contrast *Expectations III* is a work of acrylic on paper, in which the Yoruba influences can be seen. With an emphasis on anatomic human and animal features, recessive and sunken eyes, prominent noses, exaggerated foreheads, oval eyes, birds, snakes and mudfish float among the painting's dissections, where their aquatic colours are bordered by thick black lines.

In a 2005 article in *The Guardian,* journalist Molara Wood quotes Jegede at the opening of an exhibition at the October Gallery saying 'I am a political artist. There is no African alive today who is not aware of the injustices faced by our continent.' The 'injustices relate to the unequal structures of power which ensure and perpetuate Africa's subservience to the West – even in matters of the arts.'[43]

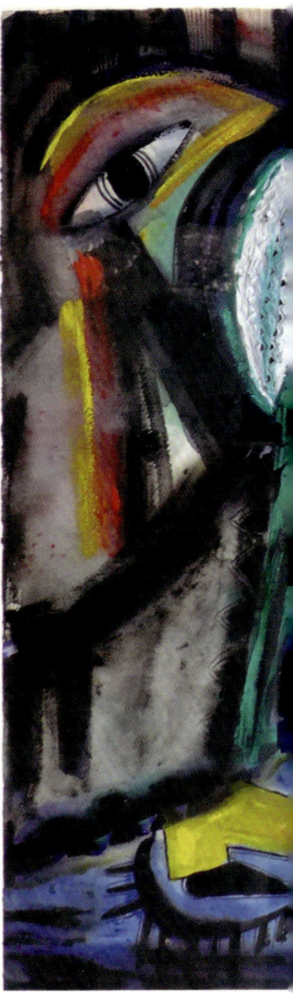

Expectations III 1994
Acrylic paint on paper
55 x 73

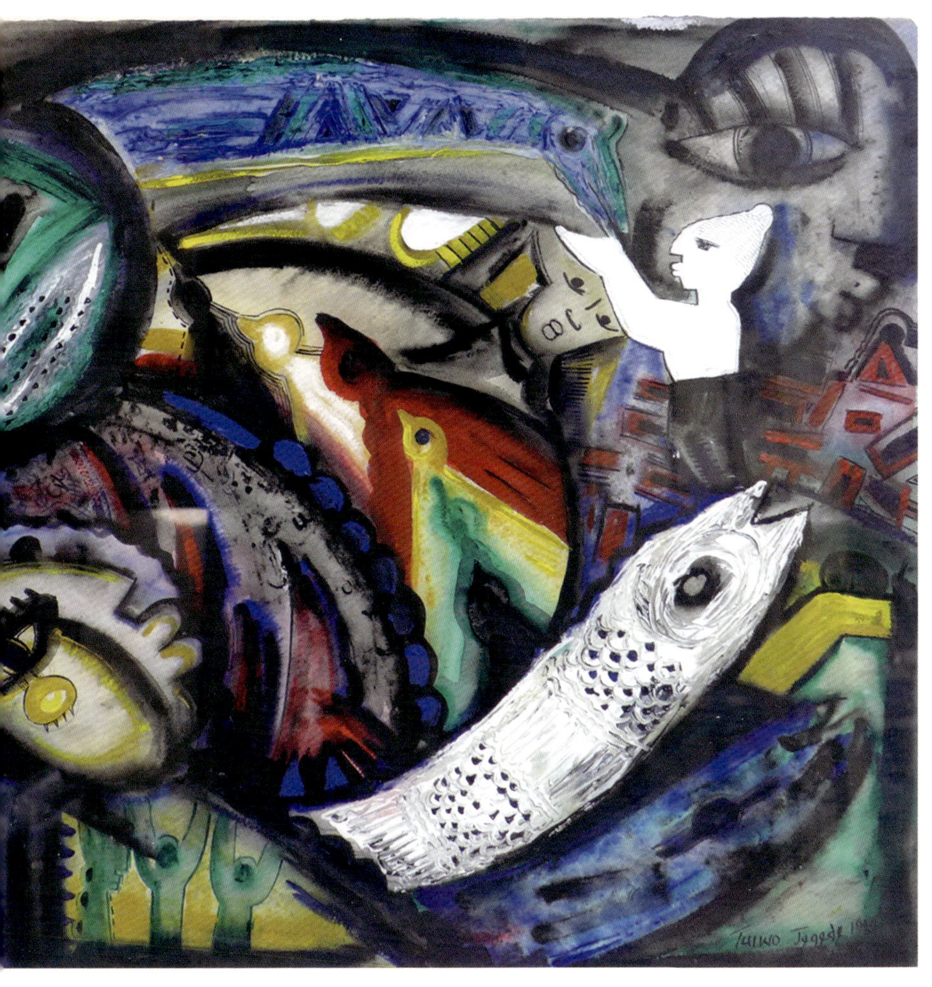

Eugene Palmer b.1955

Eugene Palmer had a different style of painting from most of his peers. While they were best known for their life-like images, his early abstract works were characterised by strident colours, and are suggestive of spiritual fantasies in the early 1980s. By the next decade, Black culture and history became more prominent in his practice.

Palmer left Jamaica for Britain with his parents in 1966. His memories of friends and family would shape his art, and the Black female in particular is a frequent exponent of his grand manner of portraiture work. He painted his mother from a photograph taken after her arrival in Britain. It was common at this time for Black immigrants who were proud of their achievements and resilience in Britain to mark their progress with studio portraiture.

Duppy Shadow 1994
Oil paint on canvas
210 x 155

The green shrubbery in *Duppy Shadow* is animated, luminous and dense, as is the woman's brown skin. 'Duppy' is a Jamaican term for an unfriendly ghost or a spirit; the woman dressed in black (the potential duppy) is standing awkwardly against the backdrop creating a sharp contrast between the figure and an iconically British landscape.

Palmer exhibited regularly in the 1980s, especially in *Artists Against Apartheid* (1985), *Caribbean Expressions in Britain* (1987) and *The Other Story* (1989). 'I see my work as participating in a cultural discourse. It is no more or less than another voice, another point of view, and another position from which to engage with that ongoing discursive process to do with asking questions about art.'[44]

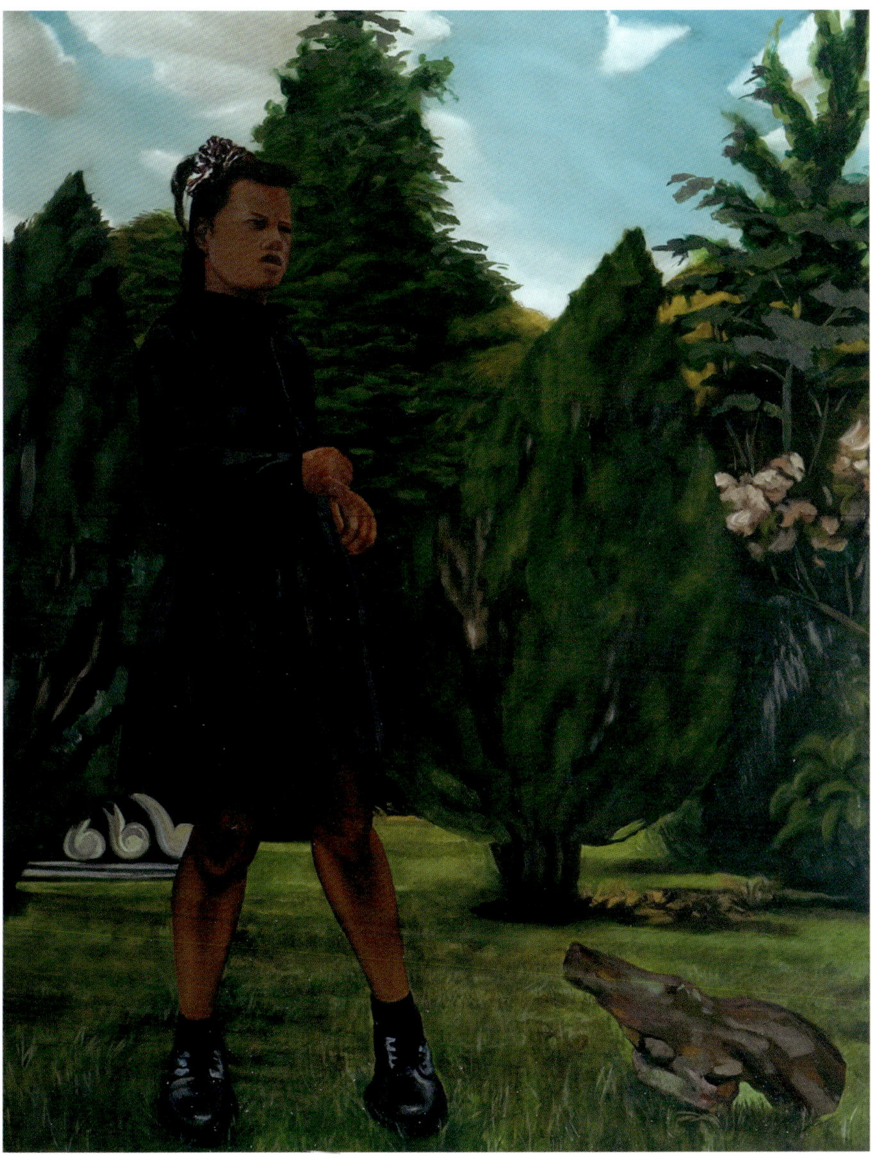

George 'Fowokan' Kelly b.1943

In his 1989 essay, sculptor and jeweller George 'Fowokan' Kelly declared; 'If African art is to be more than a few lines in a newspaper about the record price paid for a piece of "tribal art" or some other exotic curio, then we Africans will have to begin to take our art more seriously once more; if it is to have any relevance to our lives today, then we must begin to define and control it ourselves.'[45]

Jamaican-born Fowokan first encountered African sculptures in his early teens at the Horniman Museum in London, where he also came to appreciate, through photographs, the craftsmanship of African masks, spears and shields. Mostly self-taught, Fowokan would first experiment with clay and stone, but on his 1974 visit to Nigeria, on tour with the Jamaican musician Jimmy Cliff, he discovered Benin and Ife sculptures in bronze and vowed to learn how to sculpt in a similar fashion. Now known for his naturalistic busts of radical Black figures, in *Bust of Jessica Huntley* Fowokon immortalises posthumously Jessica Huntley, who co-founded one of the UK's first Black publishing houses in 1968, Bogle L'Ouverture Publications (BLP).

Bust of Jessica Huntley
1997
Iron resin and fibreglass
63 x 25 x 26

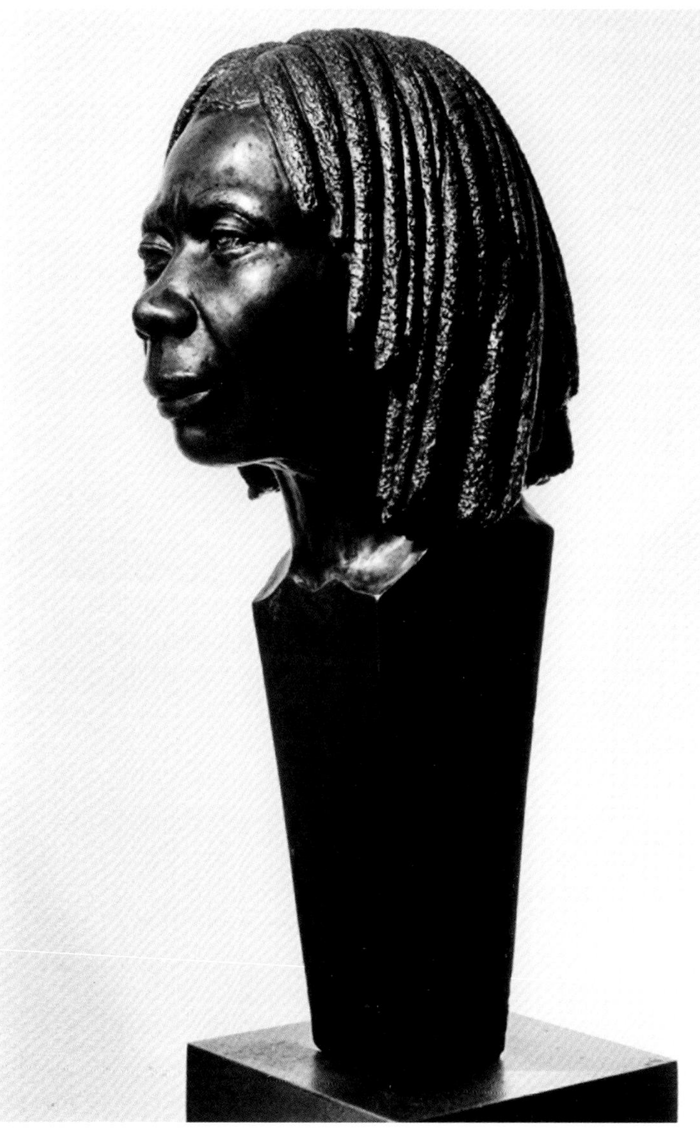

Chris Ofili b.1968

Doreen Lawrence, the mother of Stephen Lawrence – an eighteen-year-old aspiring architect who was knifed to death by a racist mob of white men at a South London bus stop in 1993 – is commemorated in Chris Ofili's large-scale coarse canvas painting *No Woman, No Cry.* A year after its creation, The Macpherson Report published the findings of a public inquiry that would go on to describe the Metropolitan Police's response to Lawrence's killing as 'marred by a combination of professional incompetence, institutional racism and a failure of leadership.' In the painting, Doreen is shedding tears, each bearing an image of her son in phosphorescent paint, amid the words 'RIP Stephen Lawrence 1974–1993.' Born in Manchester to Nigerian parents, Ofili knew that to consider history of this kind in artwork of such recent vintage was to better understand Britain's poor regard for Black lives.

Once Charles Saatchi (known to buy out entire shows of work) became the pre-eminent patron of the Young British Artists (YBAs), the group definition came to include Ofili, its only Black member (though it should be noted the artist does not self-identify as a YBA). *No Woman, No Cry* was one of the works for which Ofili won the Turner Prize that year, making him the first Black artist to win the prize, and the first painter to be awarded it in over ten years. Ofili was quoted saying: 'The way I work comes out of experimentation, but it also comes out of a love of painting, a love affair with painting.'[46]

No Woman, No Cry 1998
Oil paint, acrylic paint,
graphite, polyester resin,
printed paper, glitter,
map pins and elephant
dung on canvas
243.8 x 182.8

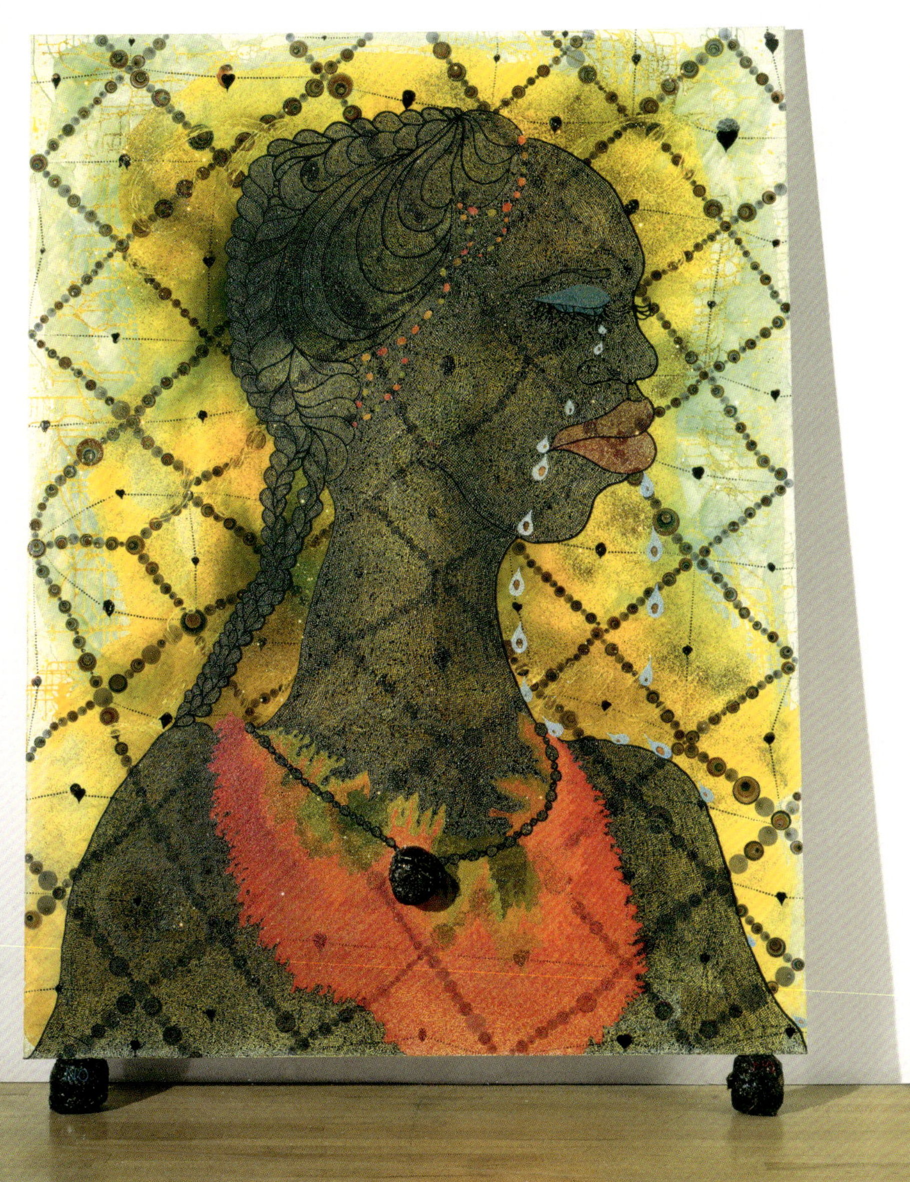

Maud Sulter 1960–2008

The title *Les Bijoux* is borrowed from Charles Baudelaire's
1857 poem about his muse, a nineteenth century
mixed-race Haitian woman named Jeanne Duval. In this
text, Baudelaire's fetishising thoughts of Duval loosely
translate to: 'My darling was naked, and knowing my
heart well. She was wearing only her sonorous jewels.
Whose opulent display made her look triumphant,
like Moorish concubines on their fortunate days.'[47]
In the series *Les Bijoux,* Maud Sulter inserted herself into
nine photographs to take the representative position
of Duval, clothed and defiant. Sulter's fine art practice
included text, photography, sound and performance.
Born in Glasgow, to Scottish and Ghanaian parents,
her lifework as a writer, curator, gallerist, publisher and
artist was definitive and lasting in equal measures.

In 1980, Sulter edited the book *Passion: Discourses in
Blackwomen's Creativity* and in the preface she opens:
'The endeavours and successes of Blackwomen's
creativity are often criticised but seldom critiqued in a
constructive upwards and outwards way. This leads to fear
of discourse and dialogue which undermines our aims and
must be countered. Discourse is a primary tool against the
weapons used to marginalise and write out of history our
contribution, she who writes herstory rewrites history.'[48]

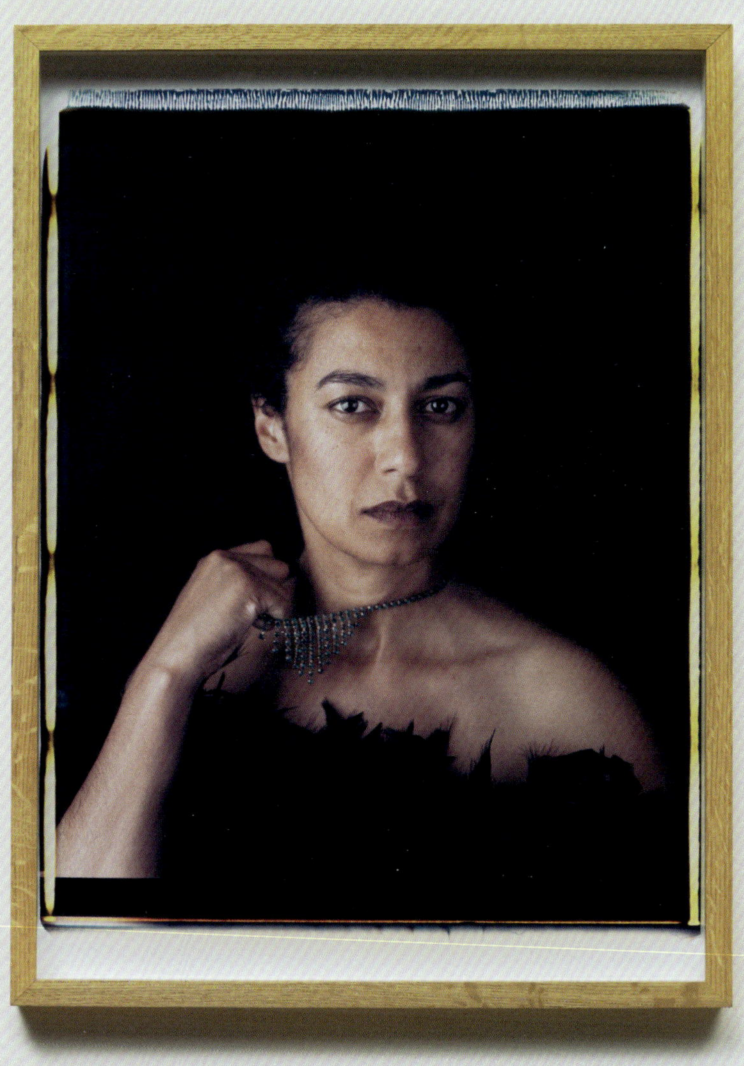

Kimathi Donkor b.1965

Kimathi Donkor was born in the UK to an Anglo-Jewish mother and Ghanaian father, but he was raised by his Jamaican and English adopted parents. Since its infancy his painting practice has functioned as a social documentation of Black lives internationally and the restaging of their histories.

In his 2005 series *Under Fire, 'Fall/Uprising'* Donkor depicts seminal scenes from 1985, a time of political insurgence for Black Britons. *Under Fire: The Shooting of Cherry Groce* re-stages the early-morning attack of an elder Black woman who was shot by a London Metropolitan Police officer during a house-raid searching for her twenty-one-year-old son. Her shooting ignited the 1981 Brixton uprising. Donkor recounts: 'On a street close to Goldsmiths – and to my own home – police raided the house of Cherry Groce, an innocent Black grandmother, shooting her and paralysing her for life. The following week, another innocent Black working-class grandmother, Cynthia Jarrett, died during a police raid on her Tottenham home. Both events were followed swiftly by local protest demonstrations. Street clashes then escalated, leading to the deaths of a policeman and a journalist. It was a moment of social unrest and personal tragedy. Working with local activists, I began to use my artistic skills to produce flyers and posters designed to help develop an organised response to abuses of power.'[49]

Under Fire: The Shooting of Cherry Groce 2005
Oil paint on canvas
121 x 182

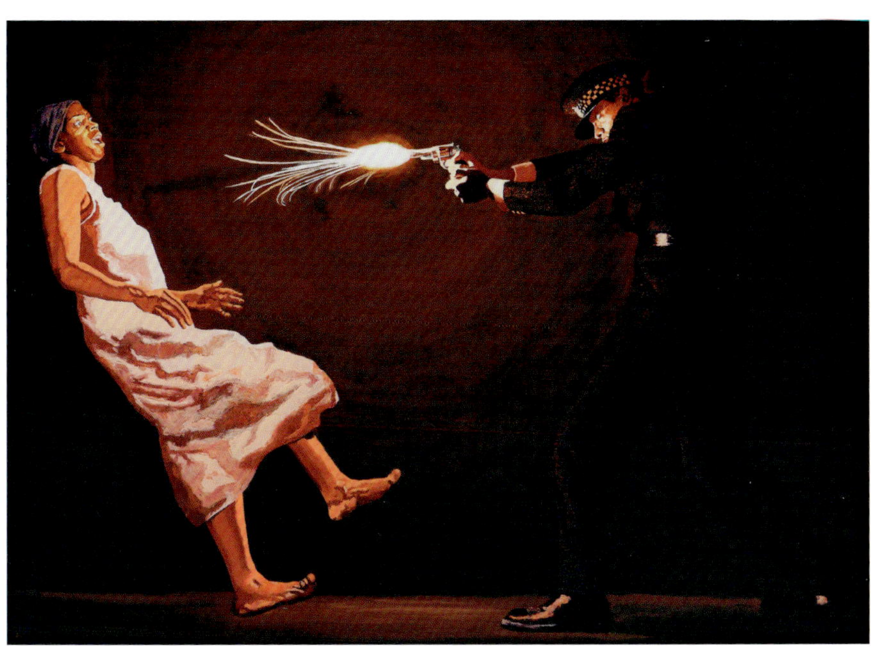

Hurvin Anderson b.1965

As the youngest in a Birmingham-based family and the only one born in the UK, Anderson admits he was 'the English boy in the Jamaican conversation'.[50] But regardless of his place of birth, Anderson had a strong affiliation with his family's native country, and the work of Jamaican figurative artist Ras Daniel Heartman in particular was an early visual influence for him, even though he wouldn't begin his career as an artist until he was in his thirties.

Jersey captures a scene at a barbershop in Jamaica void of people. Under the light of fluorescent strips you can see freshly cut tresses littered around two barber chairs, shaving clippers and spray bottles dressing the countertop. On the lightly washed blue wall, would-be posters and photographs of historical Black figures and celebrities are outlined with blocked out rectangles and squares in clusters of collages. Speaking to the diasporic cultural affirmation felt in this location, Anderson explains: 'my fascination came from remembering what it felt like to enter and be inside that space. When you walked in there were mirrors that reflected you and anyone else in the room. It was a space where you could enter, sit down, relax, and there would be a certain stillness in that.'[51]

Jersey 2008
Oil paint on canvas
250.3 x 208.3

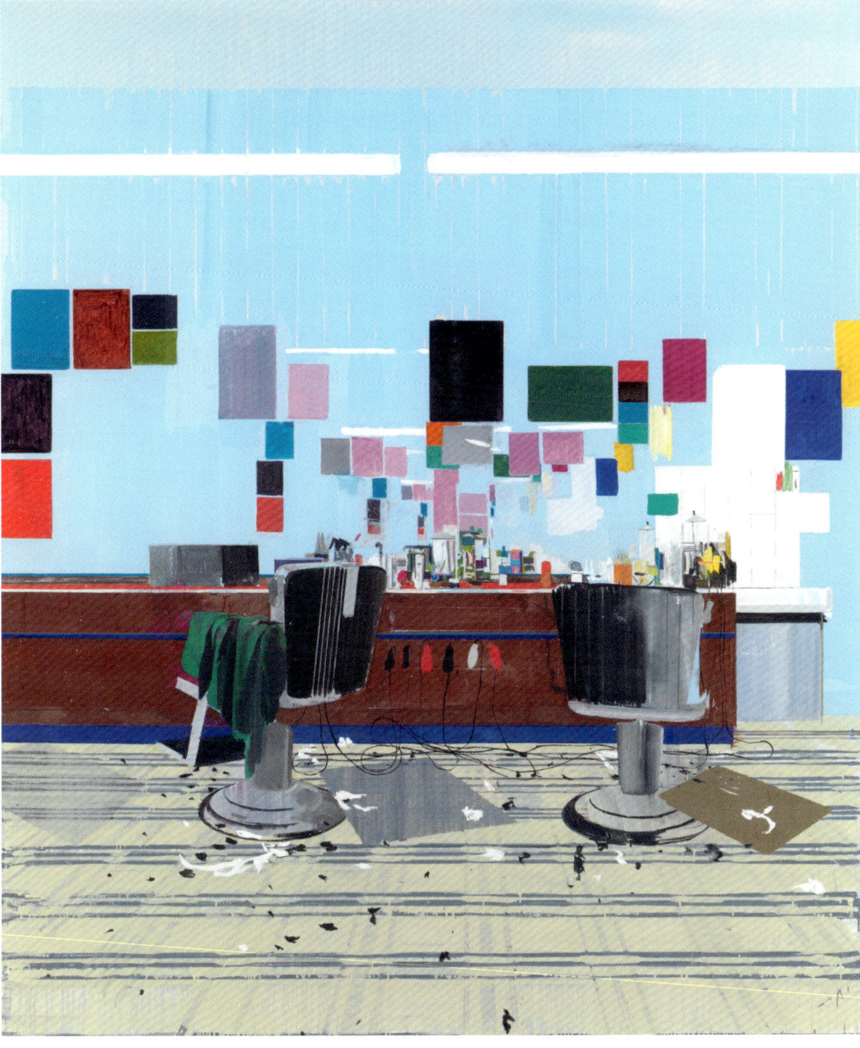

Lynette Yiadom-Boakye b.1977

In *Wrist Action* Lynette Yiadom-Boakye depicts a Black man with dark jagged hair, sitting upright with legs crossed. His white turtleneck matches the brightness of his teeth and a pink-gloved hand lays limp on his lap. Often painting her Black subjects in deep browns, the viewer is made to look closely and intently in order to construct a face.

Known for painting figures from her imagination, Yiadom-Boakye states about her mode of image-making: 'There were these ideas about how a Black body should be, should move, what Blackness means. I can divorce the work from that expectation of reality and refer to a different reality. My figures are recognisably people. One of the things people assume about my stance is that I don't want to talk about race and that somehow this isn't political. It's never been that. I just don't like being told who I am, how I should speak, what to do and how to do it. I've never needed telling.'[52]

In 2020, Yiadom-Boakye became the first Black British woman to present a solo exhibition at Tate, with a survey of her figurative oil paintings.

Wrist Action 2010
Oil paint on canvas
250 x 200

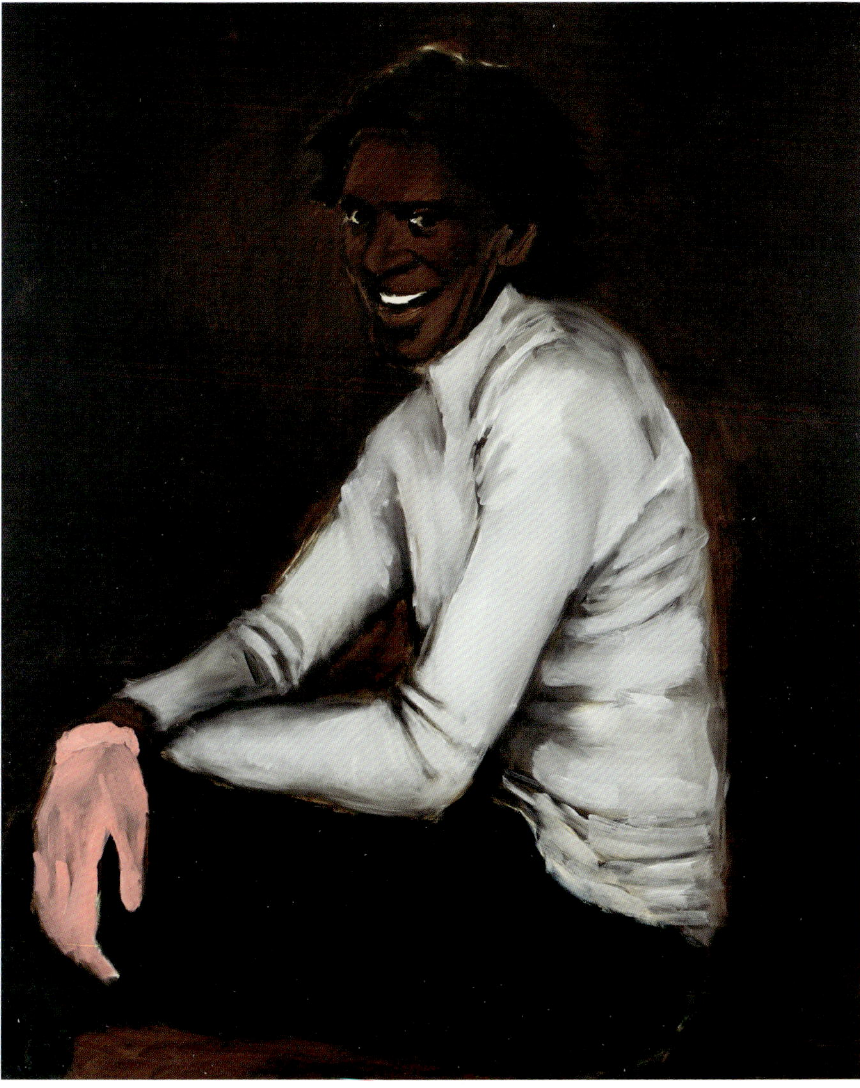

John Akomfrah b.1957

With his health in decline, the Jamaican-born academic and cultural theorist Stuart Hall (1932–2014) gave filmmaker John Akomfrah access to his personal archive to make a narrative of his life's work and presence in the UK since arriving at Oxford to study at the age of nineteen in 1951. *The Unfinished Conversation,* centered on Hall and his unique method of education for all, is a single-screen film for cinema, and has also been presented as a three-screen installation intended for display in galleries.

Ghana-born Akomfrah, the founding member of the influential Black Audio Film Collective (see also p.76) shares how he chose and adhered to the title of the work: 'The object of the exercise was to find how this process, this conversation, this unfinished dialogue between the personal and the political happened in his [Stuart Hall's] case. How does the public and the private intersect in his life, the persona that we know as Stuart Hall.'[53]

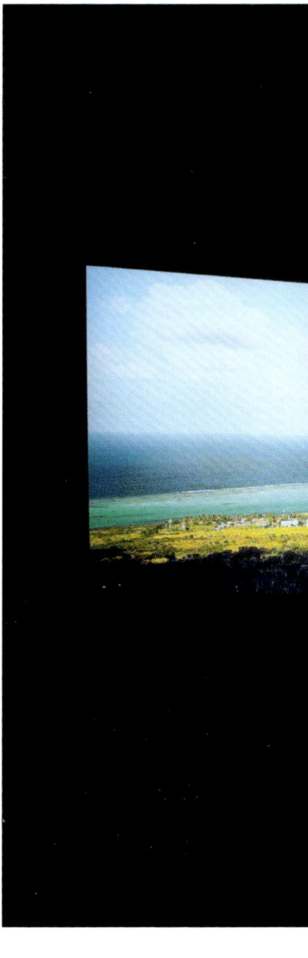

The Unfinished Conversation 2012
Video; high definition,
3 projections, colour and
sound (surround)
45 min

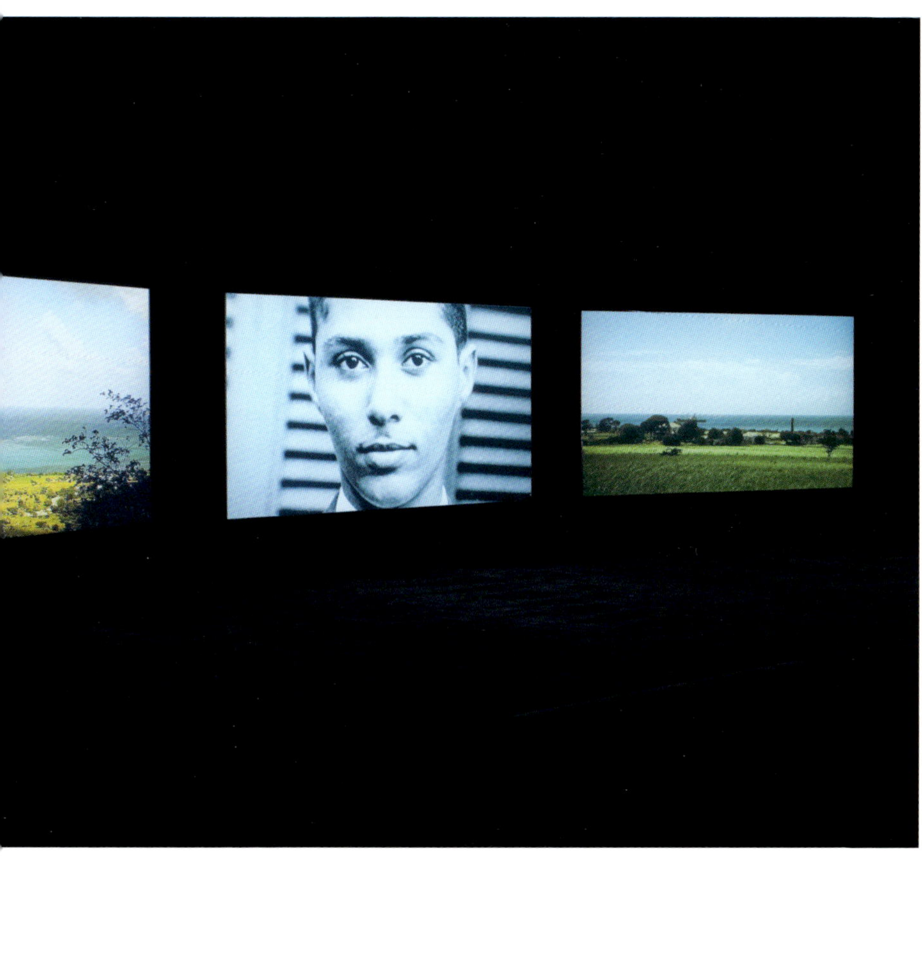

Anthea Hamilton b.1978

Anthea Hamilton's installations and bold mixed-media artworks demand attention. Facetious and impressive in concept and configuration, they serve as cultural repositories for fashion and pop icons, 1970s disco, Japanese Kabuki Theatre and architecture. More subtle than some of her more well-known works, the suspended PVC leatherette *Wrestler Kimono* is marked by red and white checks, which represent the strength of the wrestler. In the Edo period, the stronger the checks, the stronger the wrestler.

Once questioned by a reporter about the 'burden' of representing her race and gender, the London-born artist retorted: 'When something truncates the reading of someone's work, I think that's a waste of time and energy for everyone. Maybe my work isn't seen for what it is. (…) I see the point of tagging something because it's supposed to stimulate debate but it doesn't change anything for the people involved in making it. (…) I'm the first viewer. It's important what I think. It has to please me, it's how I train myself as an artist.'[54]

Wrestler Kimono 2013
PVC leatherette, silk satin
acetate, cotton and steel
on wooden base
212 x 190.3 x 43.8

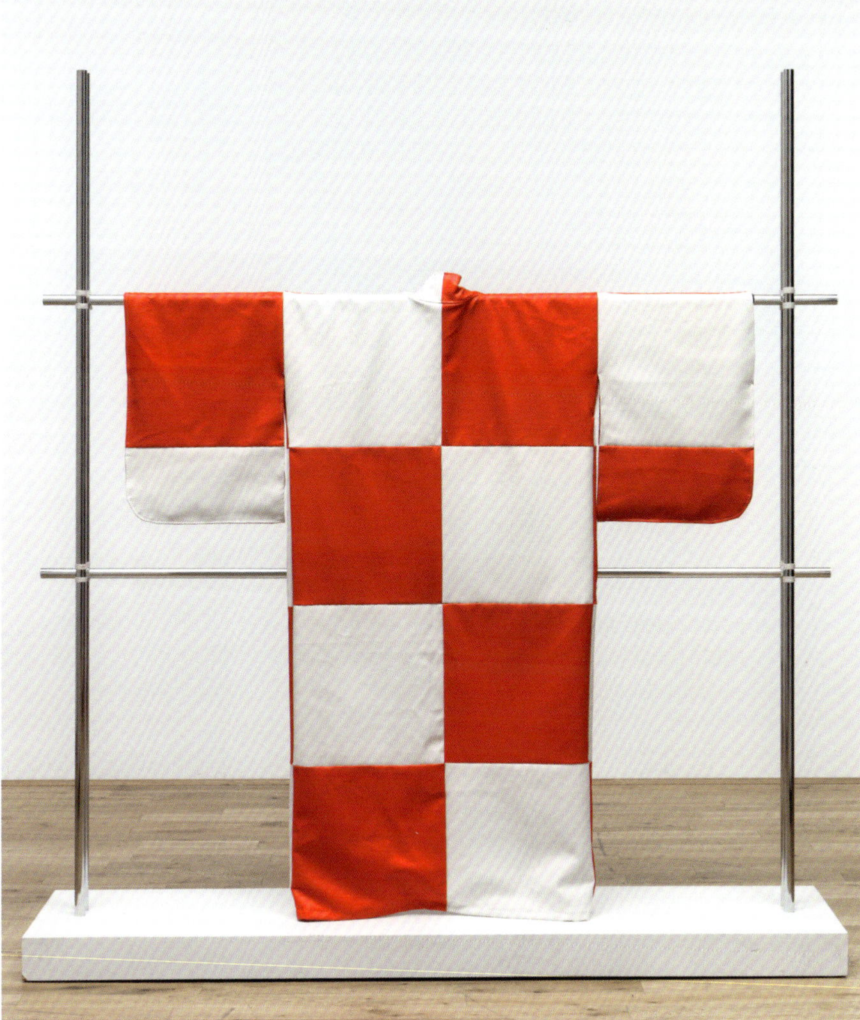

Yinka Shonibare b.1962

Born in England but raised in Nigeria, Yinka Shonibare interrogates the signifiers of ethnicity to expose the hidden presence of colonialism. Although perhaps a predictable choice, Shonibare's use of 'African' textiles made in Manchester can be considered playful and a necessary cultural reference, as exemplified in *The British Library,* an installation of over 6000 hardback books covered in wax print. Printed in gold leaf on the spine of 2700 of the books are the names of famous and unknown migrants, who have contributed to British culture and history, as well as public opposers of migration to Britain. All of the names featured are listed on the artwork's independent website.

In an interview for ART X Lagos, Nigeria's premier art fair, Shonibare states: 'People responded to my work because I was doing something that hadn't been done before. I was actually bringing something from the market into Western art galleries and I was also referencing colonialism. People were used to political art being kind of dry, boring and dull. I wanted to actually do something exciting, but which at the same time had a strong political message.'[55]

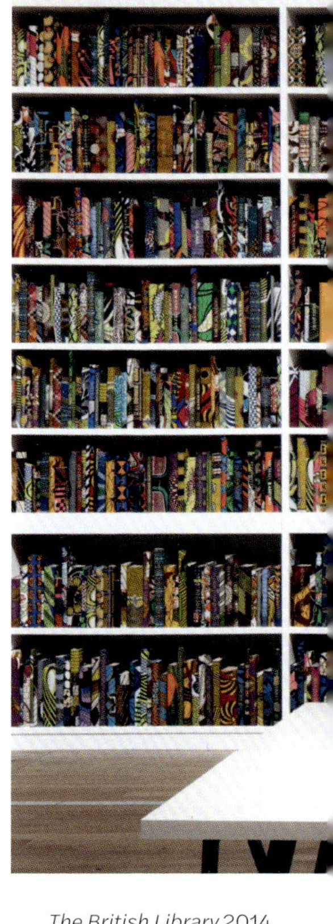

The British Library 2014
6,328 books;
Dutch wax print fabric,
gold foil, software,
networked to the
worldwide web, table
and chairs
Display dimensions
variable

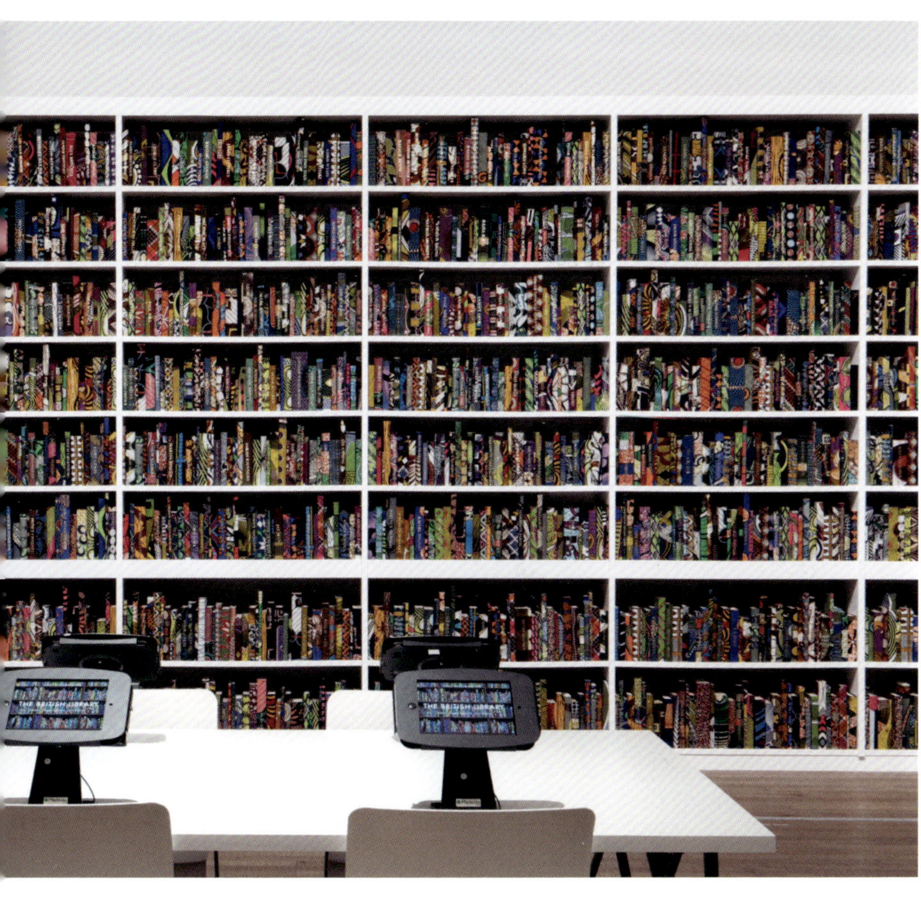

Sokari Douglas Camp b.1958

Born in Rivers State, Nigeria, Sokari Douglas Camp moved to the UK and studied fine art at the Central School of Art and Design in London. Her first solo exhibition *Alali (Festival Time)* in 1982 was held at the Africa Centre in its original Covent Garden location. Over four decades, Camp has represented both Nigeria and the UK as an internationally recognised sculptor.

The making of *Europe Supported by Africa and America* is perhaps best described by the artist: 'This piece was inspired by a drawing by William Blake with the same title. I have Africanized the figures; dressing them in cloth that could come from different parts of the world; Asia a paisley motived fabric, then a Mondrian pattern that looks like sleek building blocks to represent Europe and a woven cloth with an Igbo pattern for Africa. The women have gele head ties (this fabric is produced in Switzerland). The three graces represent women in the world resting on their laurels as humankind is holding a wreath which ends with a petrol nozzle; their backdrop is mountains and they stand gracefully on a cushion of lush grass and flowers. I think the work is international and conscious of our humanity and the coercion in working with each other and not caring for the environment. Business as usual?'[56]

Europe Supported by Africa and America 2015
Steel, abalone, copper gold and copperleaf and petrol nozzles
200 x 181 x 93

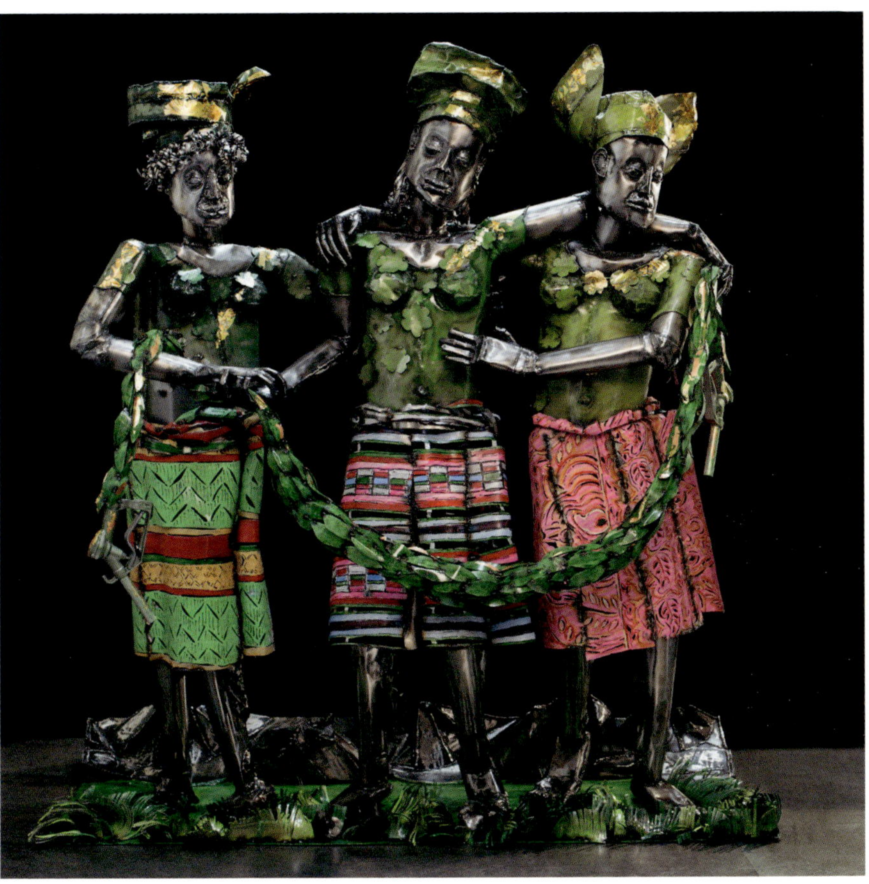

Hew Locke b.1959

Tate was made on the occasion of the Tate Britain exhibition *Artist and Empire* in 2015. It depicts Henry Tate (founder of Tate and Lyle sugar refinery company and Tate galleries) almost buried under layers of brass sugar cubes and sugar cane.

Born in Edinburgh, Hew Locke (son of artist Donald Locke) spent his formative years in Guyana, arriving just in time for Independence from Britain. Locke has been celebrated for his innovative amalgamations of history and modernity. His elaborate and embellished model naval ships rely on freighted symbolism as a way of pondering British control in war, trade and culture. The boats that frequently appear in Locke's work may have some historical background for people of African descent, but 'they are also about what is happening now in the Mediterranean, what is happening with people trying to get from Haiti to the US. History is both now and in the past.' He cites: 'one of the problems with being an artist is people want to be able to say: "He's the post-colonial guy", or "He's Mr Multicultural". I have an interest in those issues but I think the work goes beyond that. I want to make art about what is happening today.'[57]

Tate 2015
Cut and engraved brass, polished and aged with mounted digital pigment print
40.6 x 39.2 x 1.2

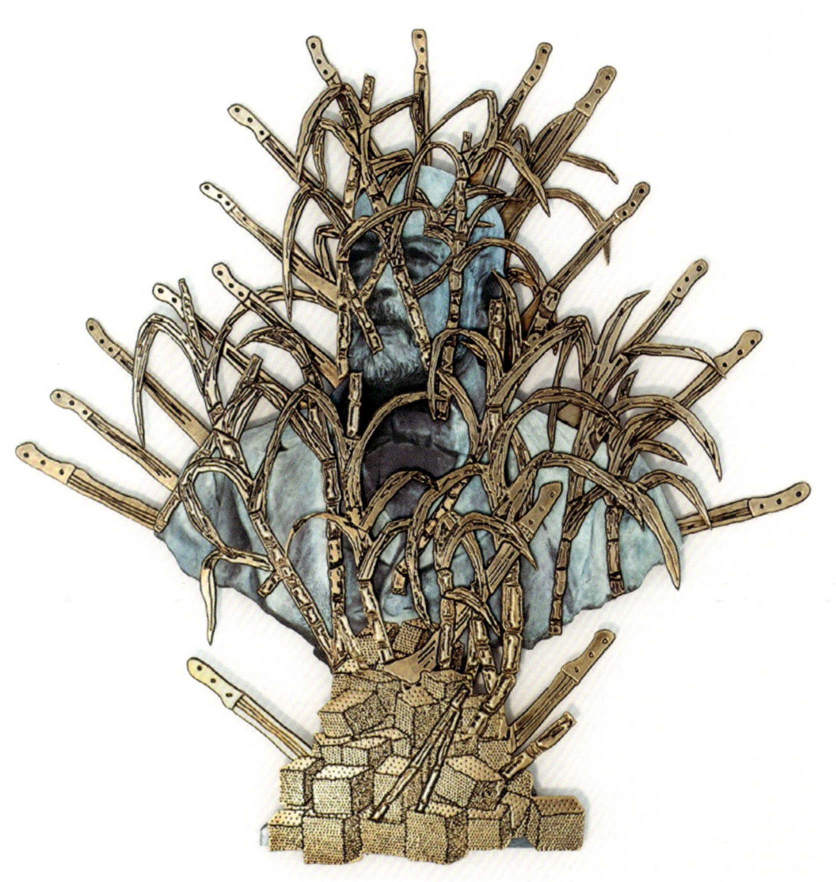

Zak Ové b.1966

Before becoming an artist, Zak Ové, whose father Horace Ové directed the feature-length film *Pressure* (1975), made videos for musicians, including Lee Scratch Perry and Chaka Demus & Pliers. Born in London to an Irish mother and Trinidadian father, Ové typically works with sculpture, film and photography to interrogate the mythologies of his Caribbean culture.

In *Moko Jumbies* two black and gold steel sculptures, male and female, hover from seven-metre high stilts. Caribbean oral traditions describe the towering stilt-walkers, Moko Jumbies, as guardians, who arrived in Trinidad from West Africa to shield the peoples of the Caribbean from the corrupt forces of the empire. Popular at Trinidad carnival, the figures parade with long colourful skirts or trousers over their stilts and masks covering their faces. It is through this act of parading that a connection can be made to ancestral powers and nature.

Ové's installation was the first by a Caribbean artist to be commissioned by the British Museum, as part of a display acknowledging Africa in 2015. It became part of the Museum's permanent collection, displayed opposite a cabinet of looted materials of African heritage, including masks made by the Yoruba and Igbo people of Nigeria, the Songye, Pende and Lega of the Democratic Republic of Congo and the Bamileke of Cameroon.

Moko Jumbies 2015
1 of 2 sculptures; steel, copper, plastic and synthetic fibres, with numerous composite objects attached, including plastic ornaments sprayed gold and textile decorations c.700 x 300

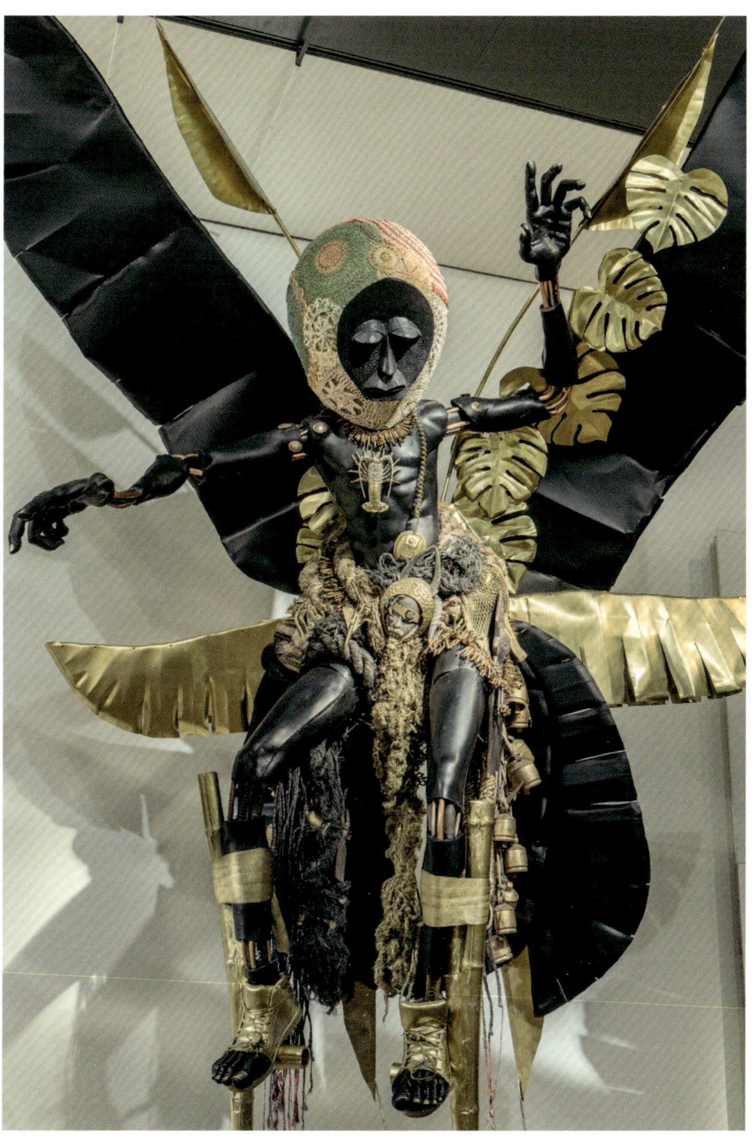

Helen Cammock b.1970

In *Slide Re-enactment (Shirley Chisholm),* Helen
Cammock has structured a mostly black-and-white
screenprinted collage with found images of Shirley
Chisholm, who was both the first Black American
woman elected to Congress and the first woman to run
as a Democrat for the US presidential election in 1972.
On the surface of the artwork is a quote 'Waiting for
the Re-enactment', as well the dictionary definition of
'Re-enactment': 'the acting out or repetition of a past
event or situation.'

Raised in London by Jamaican and English parents,
Cammock is partly influenced by the writings of, among
others, James Baldwin, Alice Walker, Frantz Fanon,
Jamaica Kincaid and Maya Angelou which, alongside her
own, are incorporated into her poetic posters and films.
When speaking of her archival research, Cammock reveals:
'He's [Baldwin] always there, he's always in my head
and because I became more interested in ideas around
intersectionality, for me he represents that in a key way:
the way he talks about queerness, the way he talks about
Blackness, the way he sees his role as an artist but also an
activist. It speaks to me, and other people are now reading
him and seeing the relevance of what he's saying in the
current context we're living in, or singing, it forms the core.
(...) Even though I say everything comes from writing,
I could never lose the visual because it does something
completely different. It either changes the meaning of
what's being said in the text or adds another layer to it.'[58]

In 2019 Cammock was awarded the Turner Prize alongside
her three fellow nominees.

*Slide Re-enactment
(Shirley Chisholm)* 2017
1 of 3 screenprints
on paper 100 x 70

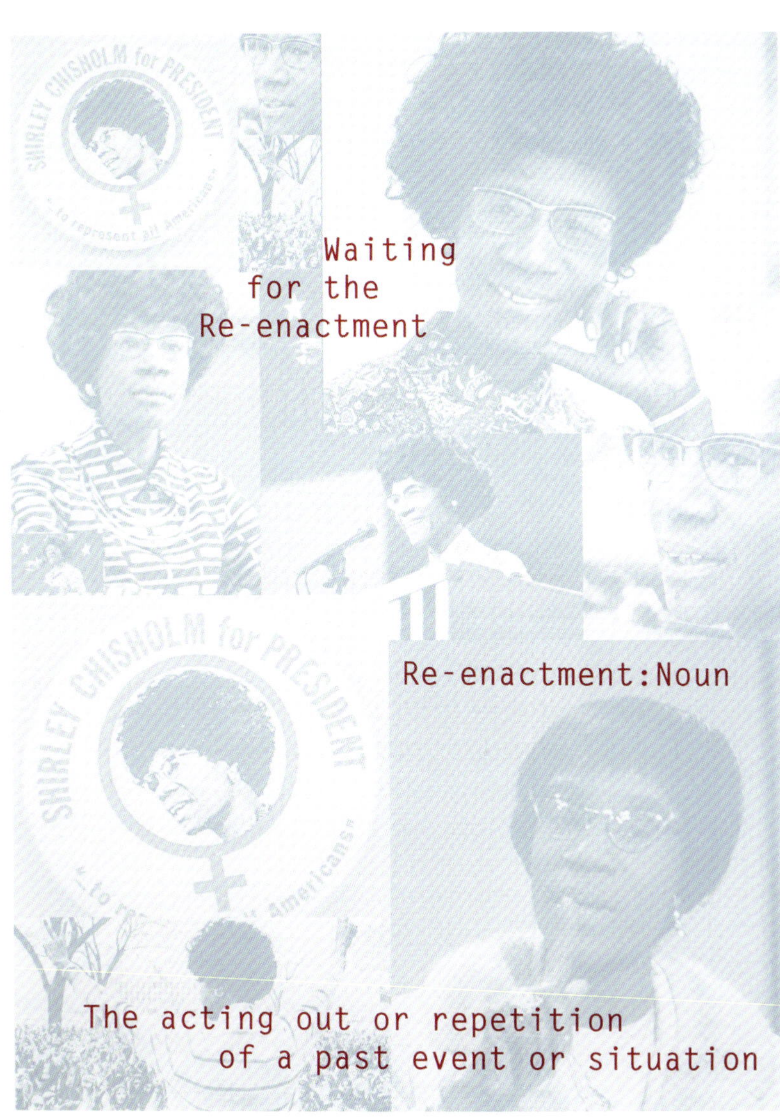

Waiting
for the
Re-enactment
Re-enactment:Noun
The acting out or repetition
of a past event or situation
SHIRLEY CHISHOLM for PRESIDENT
"...to represent all Americans"

Barbara Walker b.1964

Barbara Walker's figurative drawings and paintings largely include family, friends and neighbours in Birmingham. Given her Jamaican parentage, Walker's referential account of contributions of soldiers from the British West India Regiment during the First World War seems fitting. In *Parade*, Black soldiers, drawn from archival photographs, stand in two lines dutifully while being briefed by their white commander, whose figure is imposed onto the page but remains invisible.

Walker offers this short lesson: 'At the outbreak of WW1, thousands of West Indians volunteered to join the British army on the basis that, if they showed their loyalty to the King, they would be treated as equals. However, in the beginning, only white soldiers were allowed to fight, so the West Indians were relegated to carrying out arduous physical tasks such as loading ammunition, laying electrical wires and digging trenches for their white colleagues. I intend to challenge and then revise history in order to make the men and women from the colonial empire visible, validated and centre stage where they belong.'[59]

Parade 2018
Graphite on embossed
paper 51 x 61

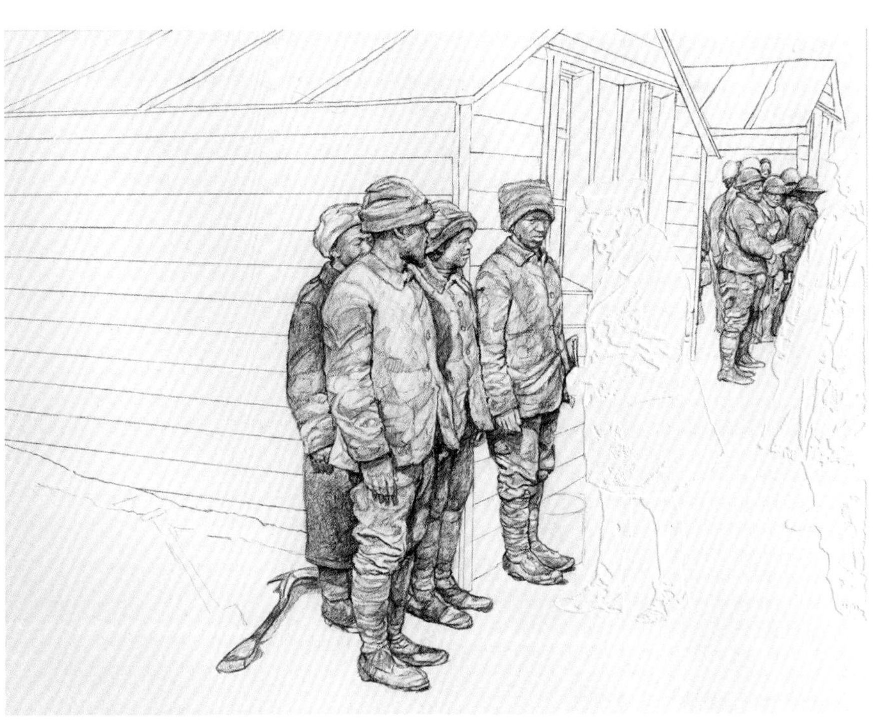

Dave Lewis b.1962

My Father's Land is a series of fiction, presenting an
alternative reality where photographer Dave Lewis is
a native of Grenada and not living in the UK. In this
scenario, he would be surrounded by lush green
mountains, dense vegetation and other tropical traits
– a good exchange for the cold and damp English air.

Lewis explains, 'Although in some way I possess a partial
insider knowledge through my heritage, I am an outsider
who grew up largely outside the Caribbean – there is a
dissonance in being accepted, and in my own acceptance
of the realities of life and living in my parents' place of
birth. This is the space of liminality: the coming together
of two (or more) different positions and perspectives
changed and charged by influences to create a culturally-
hybrid being and set of responses.'[60]

Lewis was an exhibiting artist at the Grenada Pavilion at
the Venice Biennale in 2019.

From the series
My Father's Land 2018
Digital C-type print on
paper 198 x 112

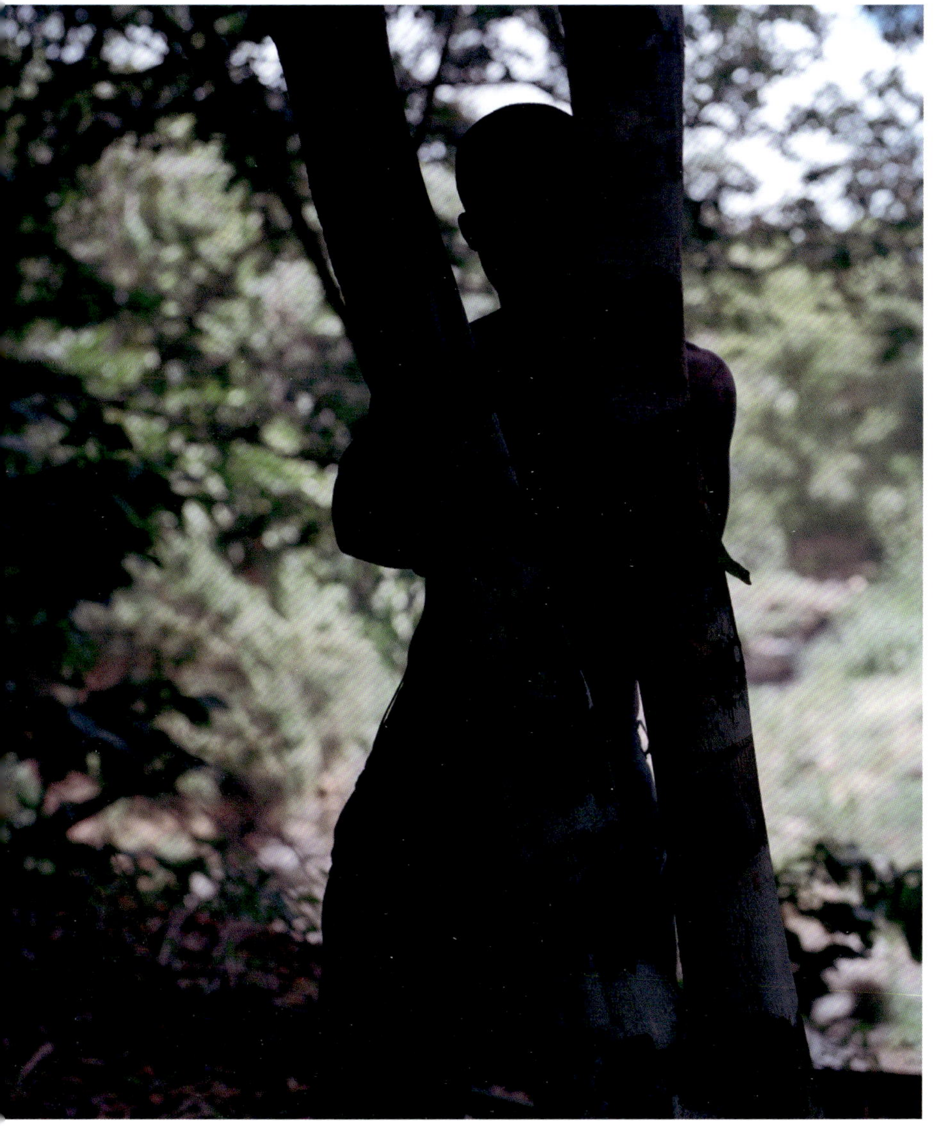

Denzil Forrester b.1956

Blended hues of middle-to-dark purple, blues and white set the tone of the midnight revellers in Denzil Forrester's nightclub scene, *Duppy Deh.* The artist explains: 'In 1980, I started going to all-night "blues" clubs. The music playing in these clubs [was] Reggae which generated particular dance movements and specialised clothing, all of which plays a part in my painting. In these clubs, city life is recreated in essence: sounds, lights, police sirens, bodies pushing and swaying back and forth. It's a continuation of city life with some spiritual fulfilment.'[61]

Grenada-born Forrester, who arrived in London in 1976, would act as a surveyor, sketching the live scenes in Jamaican blues parties and shebeens, and turning to a new blank page every few minutes, in sync with the changing of records. Black Londoners were regularly refused entry to pubs and dances in the 1980s, and so a large portion of the city was closed off to them. More than a colourful immortalisation of London nightlife, Forrester's work is a historical record of a burgeoning Windrush generation and their children who were fashioning the styles and sensibilities of a new Black British culture.

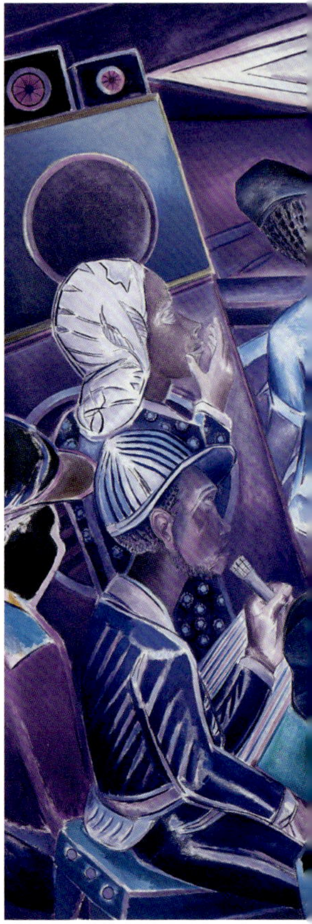

Duppy Deh 2018
Oil paint on canvas
201 x 305

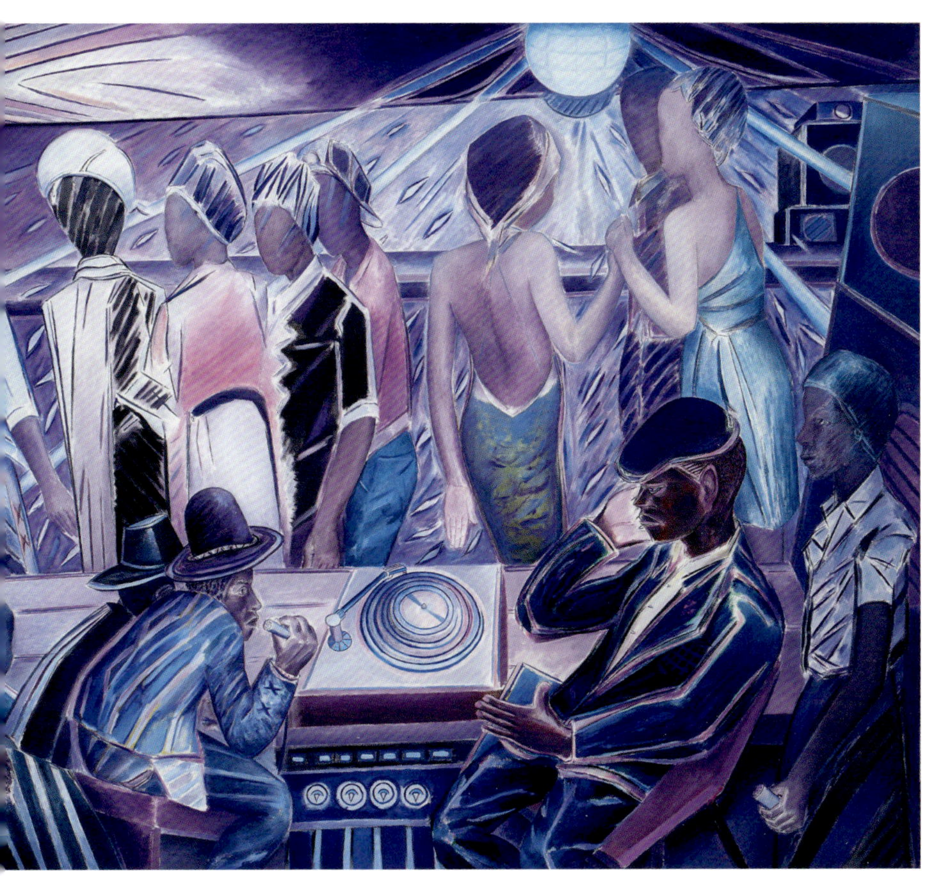

Claudette Johnson b.1959

Figurative artist Claudette Johnson, born to Jamaican parents, first saw Picasso's *Les Demoiselles d'Avignon* 1907 in reproduction as a Fine Art student, and quickly noticed his use of African imagery. In *Standing Figure with African Masks,* using a small mirror placed on a chair in her east London studio, Johnson painted herself with a large exposed belly drawn with pastel and gouache on paper looking past the frame. As in Picasso's original, abstracted figures make up the background.

In her artist statement for her first solo exhibition *Push Back the Boundaries* in 1990, Johnson proudly asserted: 'I am a Blackwoman and my work is concerned with making images of Blackwomen. Sounds simple enough – but I'm not interested in portraiture or its tradition. I'm interested in giving space to Blackwomen presence. A presence that has been distorted, hidden and denied. I'm interested in our humanity, our feelings and our politics; somethings that have been neglected.'[62]

Standing Figure with African Masks 2018
Pastel and gouache on paper 151.5 x 122

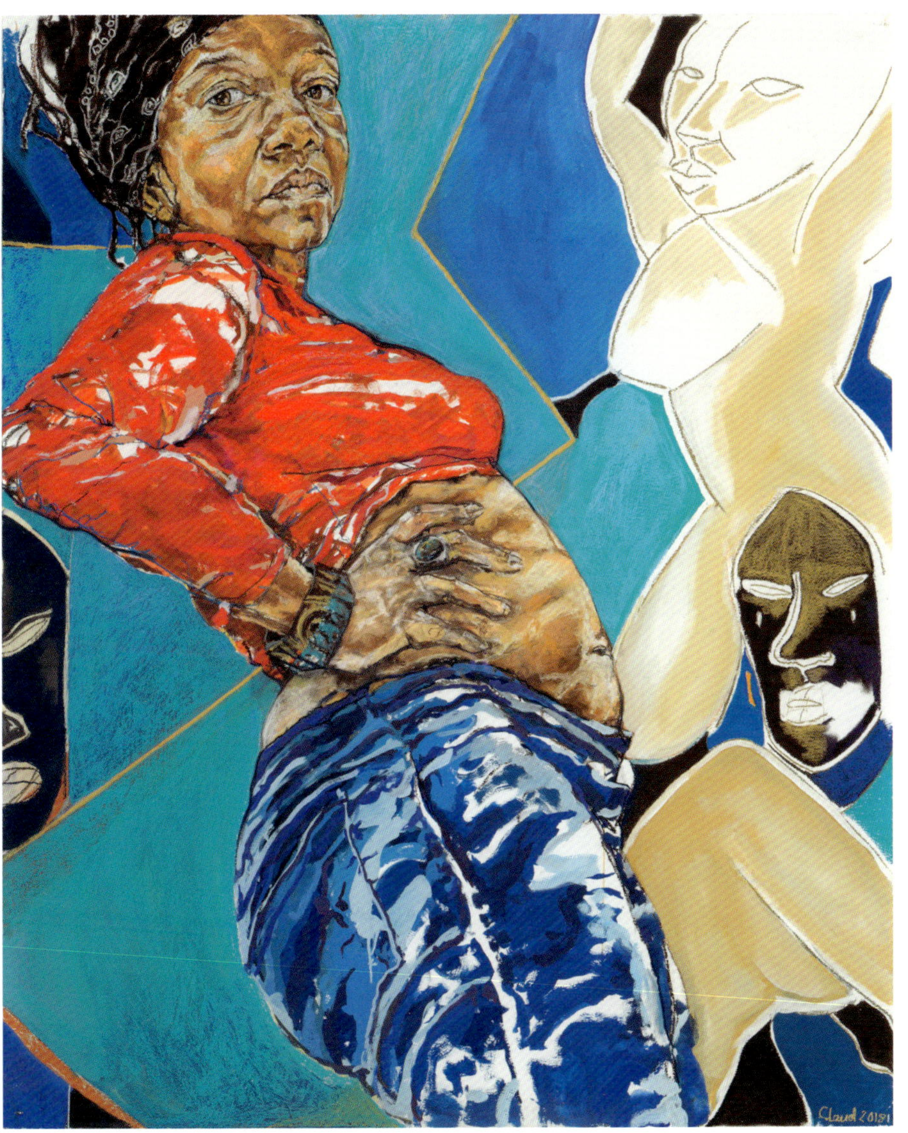
Claud 2018

Phoebe Boswell b.1982

The Space Between Things is a panoramic and minutely detailed self-portrait that Kenyan-born Phoebe Boswell produced in willow charcoal over the course of three weeks. The artist's nude body elongates, duplicates and contorts in a way that is both impressive and titillating; she twists and bends but does not break.

The work was created after a blunt trauma to the face in 2017 caused Boswell's eye to rupture, instigating sudden sight loss and implicating her otherwise healthy heart. Initially, this accidental but brutal disruption to Boswell's physical and emotional health required her to turn inwards to recuperate and eventually bare her new self through her art-making. Since then, the multimedia artist has had to learn how to work with her materials again. She shared: 'I can't really see on my right side, so trust in a physical sense was a really difficult thing and trusting that the audience would hold the grief was a big thing for me. I actually have to trust that the audience will care for me and the work... With the right team around your work, it can be the most healing and transformative thing you can do.'[63]

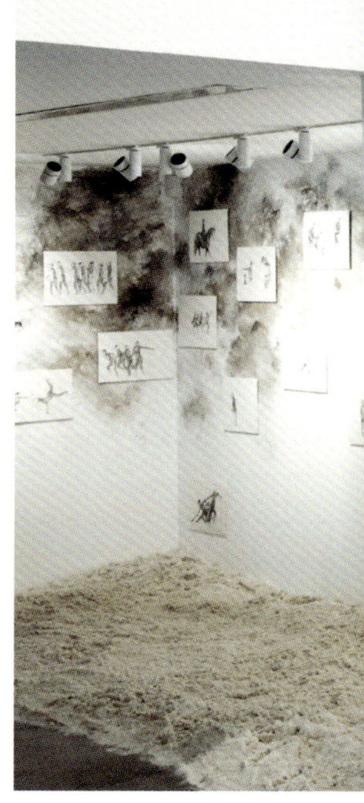

The Space Between Things
2018
Charcoal
Dimensions variable

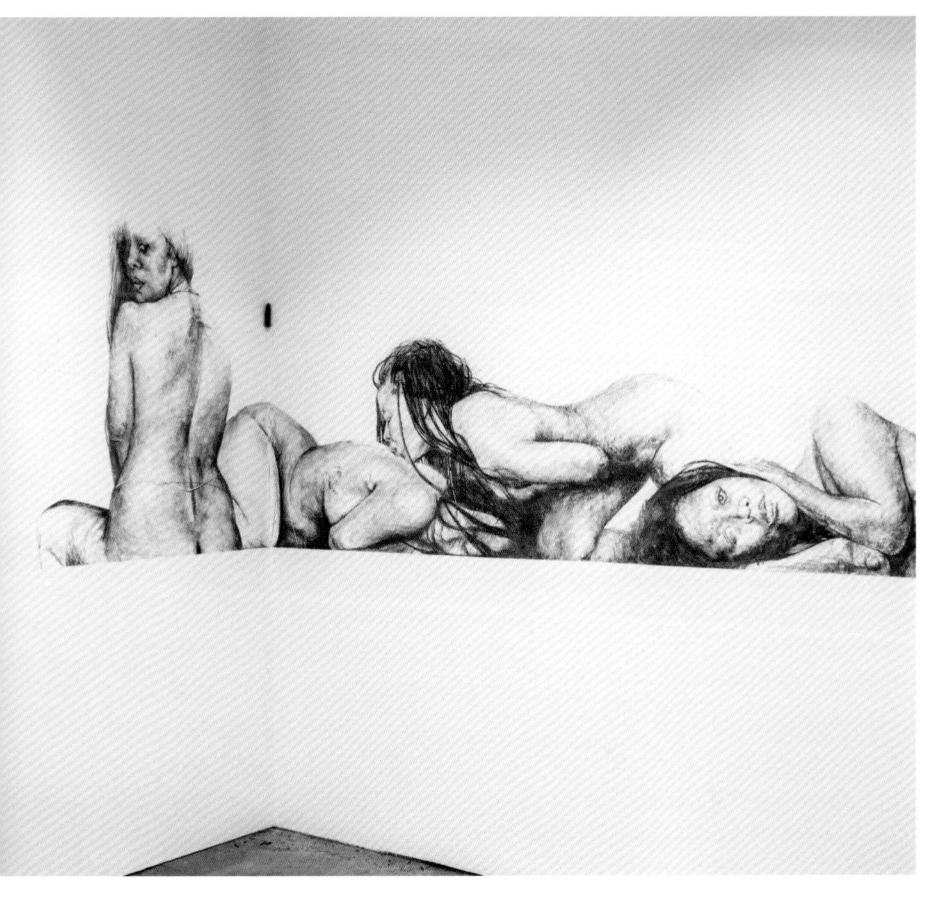

Paul Dash b.1946

In *Pick O' The Crop,* Paul Dash commemorates Foreday
Morning, a pre-dawn street fete that acts as a precursor
to the Grand Kadooment, also known as Crop Over in
Barbados. In this oil painting, a mass of brightly-dressed
and brown-skinned revellers mark the 200-year tradition
of former enslaved Bajans who would celebrate the end
of the sugarcane harvest.

Dash arrived in England from Barbados at the age of
eleven, and would go on to become a committee
member and one of the younger artists of the Caribbean
Artists Movement (CAM). When reflecting on his time
in CAM, he said: 'It [Caribbean Artists Movement] made
me aware – because don't forget, I was isolated in this
world of mainstream European painting and sculpting.
It introduced me to Black painters, artists and
intellectuals – the heavyweights at that time, some of
them. And it helped me to look at myself and to question
myself: what I was trying to do with my work.'[64]

Despite presenting in group exhibitions frequently in
the 1970s, Dash did not have a solo show until 2019,
at 198 Contemporary Arts and Learning, London.

Pick O' The Crop 2018–21
Oil paint on canvas
127 x 102

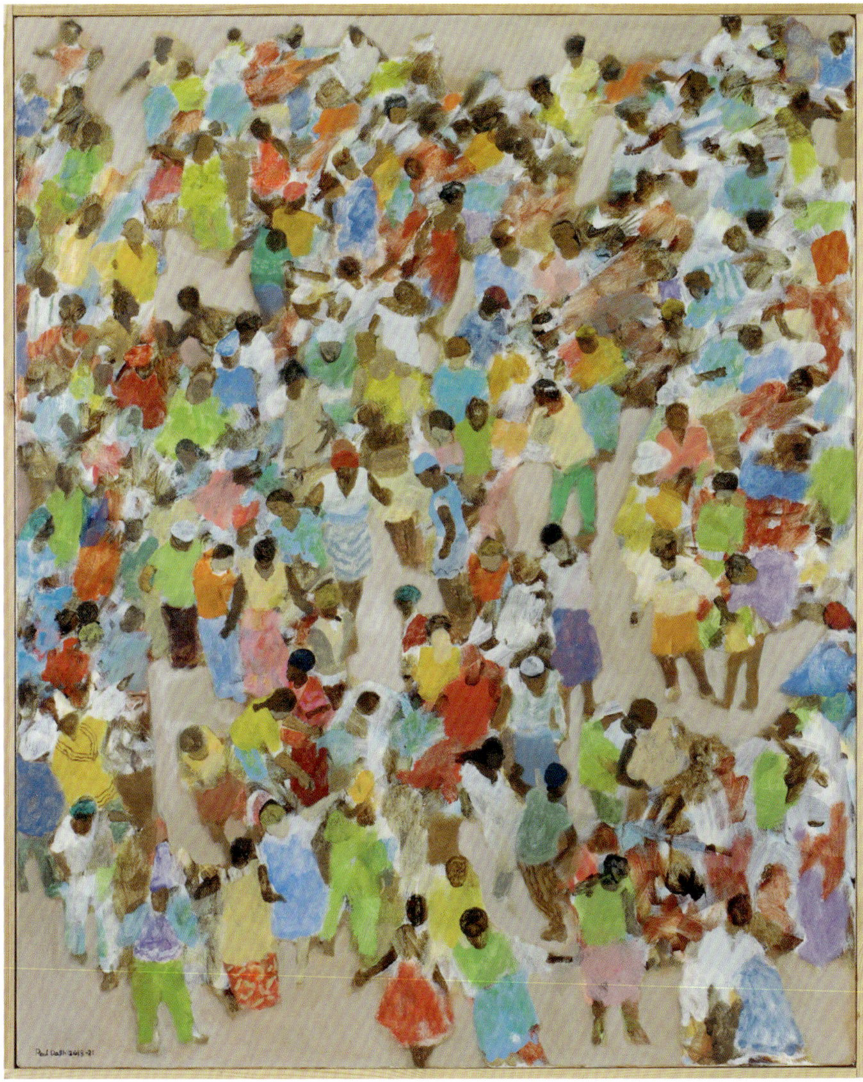

Larry Achiampong b.1984

British-born Larry Achiampong uses performance, film
and sound as a medium for his interpersonal explorations.
The artist's ongoing series of C-type prints, *Speckle,* are
taken from his Ghanaian family's photo albums.
In *Speckle #1,* the faces of four Black women are blotted
out with opaque black circles; they have no facial features
except for pursed red lips – which could be mistaken for
the racist minstrelsy of Black Americans popularised in
early nineteenth-century American theatre. Three of the
women are standing in a lively pose, clearly in a social-
setting, with Guinness bottles in view, shattering any
sinister association with caricatures and instead are a
loving reference to familial events in Ghana that have
travelled with its diaspora.

Achiampong relates his role as artist to that of Anansi,
a character in Ghanaian folklore: 'Most people especially
from a western point of view know Anansi as just a spider,
but Anansi is the shapeshifter, the spider just happens
to lend itself to particular folklore. So I like to always
imagine a position similar to that of Anansi's in painting.
Opening up different situations, different moments and
then kind of pulling the rug under the table and moving
onto something else. Like with the beats, then all of a
sudden there's the video or the photography. It's like
"catch me if you can".'[65]

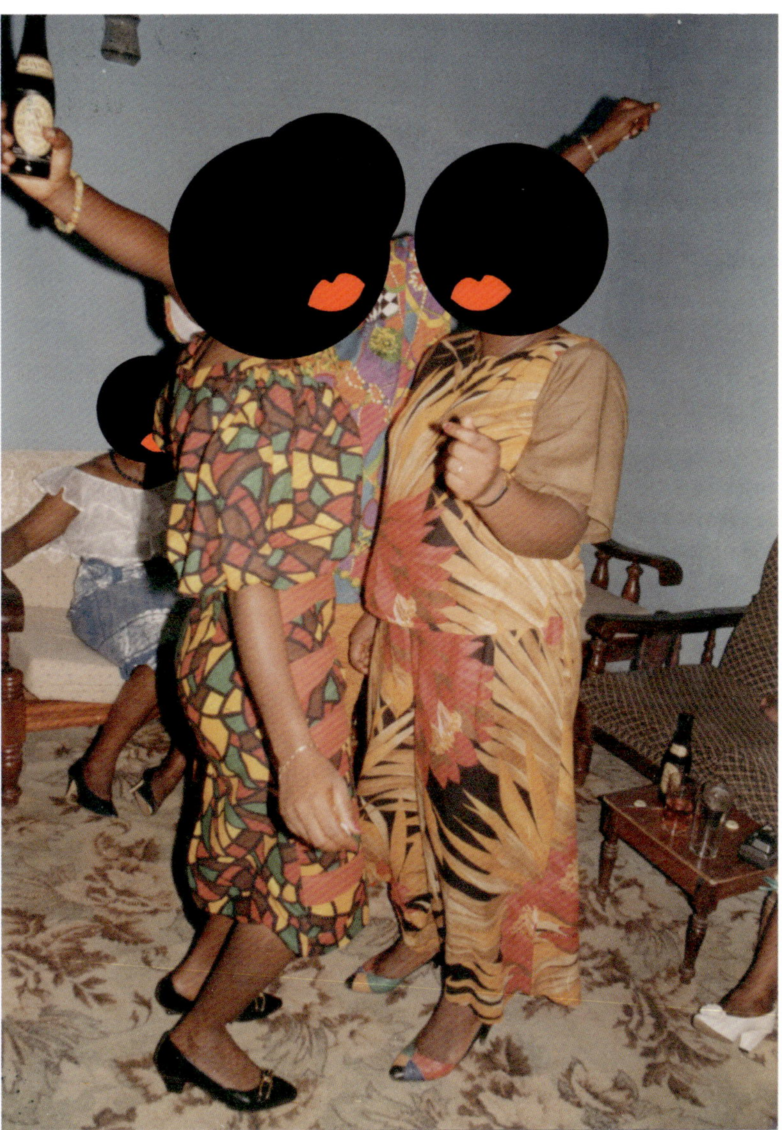

Alberta Whittle b.1980

RESET opens with Alberta Whittle directing the viewer through meditation and deep-breathing exercises. Informed by the writings of queer theorist, Eve Kosofsky Sedgwick and cultural theorist Paul Gilroy, the film features a cabal of writers, performers and musicians who Whittle regards as collaborators.

Filmed across multiple locations, including Barbados, South Africa and the United Kingdom, the Scottish-Bajan multidisciplinary artist, who uses performance, film and print in her practice, took inspiration from multiple sources, people and places to consider avenues for rest and stillness for marginalised and exploited groups who experience public trauma with little professional support. She elaborates: '"*RESET*"'s soundscape, visual textual layers, choreography, performance and editing were each inspired by Gilroy's research on antiphony, which my collaborators and I used to develop the material in the film. In order to manifest antiphony as a methodological device, I began sharing memories, ideas, hopes, stories and recordings with my friend Yves B Golden. She then composed a score called "Maroon Rage" that became the spine of "*RESET*", from which Ama Josephine could begin work on "On Touching". These phenomenal works became entangled audio and written scores for two collaborators and players – Mele Broomes and Sekai Machache – to root their performances in.'[66]

Whittle, also a researcher and curator, was selected to represent Scotland at the Venice Biennale in 2022.

RESET 2020
4K and HD video
32 min

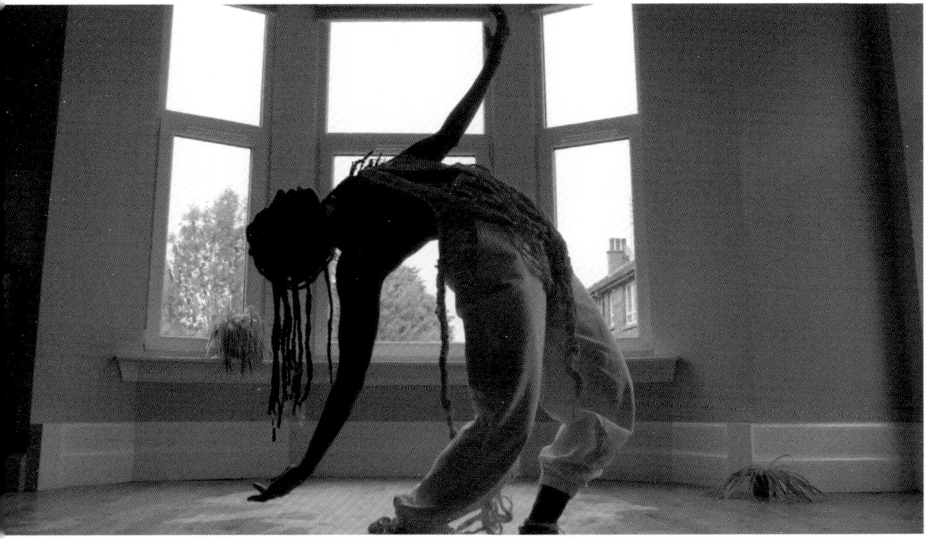

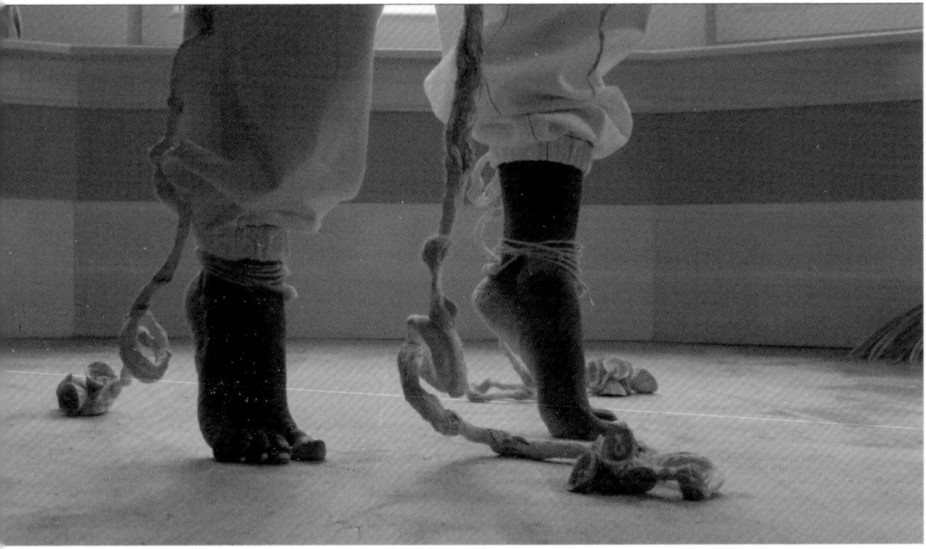

Notes

p.7: Frank Bowling, *Diaspora Artists*: http://new.diaspora-artists.net/display_item.php?id=35&table=artists, accessed September 2021.

DEFINING BLACK BRITISH ART, p.9–27

1 Rasheed Araeen and Eddie Chambers, 'Black art: A discussion', *Third Text*, vol.2, no.5, 1988, pp.51–77.

2 Mark Sealy, 'Portfolio: Rotimi Fani-Kayode – Desire in exile', *Tate Etc*, 26 October 2018: https://www.tate.org.uk/tate-etc/issue-44-autumn-2018/portfolio-rotimi-fani-kayode-desire-exile-mark-sealy, accessed July 2021.

3 'The Tate galleries and slavery': https://www.tate.org.uk/about-us/history-tate/tate-galleries-and-slavery, accessed July 2021.

4 'The Place is here': https://www.nottinghamcontemporary.org/whats-on/the-place-is-here/, accessed July 2021.

5 *Heart in Exile*, exh. cat., London 1983, p.4.

6 *Black Film Review*, vol.2, no.2, Spring 1986, p.6.

7 'Black Chronicles': https://www.npg.org.uk/whatson/blackchronicles/explore/autograph-abp, accessed July 2021.

8 'Behind the Hype': http://www.behindthehype.com/blog/movie-reviews/documentary-review/jean-michel-basquiat-the-radiant-child, accessed July 2021.

9 Paul Gilroy, 'Cruciality and the frog's perspective: An agenda of difficulties for the black arts movement in Britain', *Third Text*, vol.2, issue 5, 1988, pp.33–44.

10 Kobena Mercer, 'Black art and the burden of representation', in *Welcome to the Jungle: New Positions in Black Cultural Studies*, Abingdon, Oxfordshire 1994, p.235.

WORKS, p.30–153

1 Anne Walmsley, *The Caribbean Artists Movement 1966–1972: A Literary and Cultural History*, London 1992, p.82.

2 This sentiment from McNish is often quoted, though it has not been possible to identify the original source.

3 'Victory for a "gifted artist of colour"', *The Telegraph*: https://www.telegraph.co.uk/culture/art/artsales/9923044/Victory-for-a-gifted-artist-of-colour-79.html, accessed July 2021.

4 'Uzo Egonu 1931–1996', *Third Text*, vol.10, issue 36, 1996, pp.105–6.

5 Eddie Chambers, 'Painting of the Week:105': https://theibtaurisblog.com/2014/11/14/painting-of-the-week105/, accessed July 2021.

6 '"We have to study you in order to survive": Horace Ové on Black and white Britain': https://www.bfi.org.uk/sight-and-sound/interviews/horace-ove-interview-pressure-race-britain, accessed July 2021.

7 Letter from the artist to Tate curator, Andreas Leventis, 13 December 2009: https://www.tate.org.uk/art/artworks/locke-trophies-of-empire-t14319, accessed July 2021.

8 Walmsley 1992, p.83.

9 Ashleigh Kane, 'Documenting London's African Caribbean funerals', *Dazed*, 6 November 2014: https://www.dazeddigital.com/photography/article/22362/1/documenting-london-s-african-caribbean-funerals, accessed July 2021.

10 'Winston Branch: on Ju Ju birds and never staying still', *Art UK*, 15 January 2018: https://artuk.org/discover/stories/winston-branch-on-ju-ju-birds-and-never-staying-still, accessed July 2021.

11 Dennis Morris, *Growing Up Black*, London 2012, p.118.

12 From Alison Donnell and Sarah Lawson Welsh (eds), *The Routledge Reader in Caribbean Literature*, London and New York 1996, p.349.

13 'Face in the Crowd' – Vanley Burke returns to his photograph of Handsworth's Africa Liberation Day, 1977: https://www.bbc.co.uk/sounds/play/b0b6phll, accessed July 2021.

14 BBC Radio 4 documentary 'Face in the Crowd': https://www.bbc.co.uk/programmes/b0b6phll, accessed September 2021.

15 *The Pan-Afrikan Connection*, exh. cat., Nottingham 1983, p.6: https://issuu.com/blkres/docs/midland_group, accessed July 2021.

16 'The Godfather of Black British Film', 1 November 2007: https://ricenpeas.com/docs/menelick_shabaz.html, accessed July 2021.

17 Celeste-Marie Bernier, *Stick to the Skin: African American and Black British Art, 1965–2015*, Berkeley, CA 2019, p.60.

18 Bill Ming: http://www.billming.com/sculpture.php, accessed July 2021.

19 Art UK: https://artuk.org/discover/artworks/a-lesson-in-trust-257667, accessed July 2021.

20 Maud Sulter, *Passion: Discourses on Blackwomen's Creativity*, Chatham, Medway 1990, p.63.

21 Jayne Haynes, 'Why Handsworth Riots are being revisited with giant billboards across Birmingham', *Birmingham Mail*, 12 March 2019: https://www.birminghammail.co.uk/news/midlands-news/handsworth-riots-being-revisited-giant-15928028, accessed July 2021.

22 'Photographer in Focus: Pogus Caesar': https://www.npg.org.uk/collections/about/photographs-collection/photographers-in-focus/photographer-in-focus-pogus-caesar, accessed September 2021.

23 The exhibition *Caribbean Expressions in Britain* took place at Leicestershire Museum and Art Gallery, Leicester, 16 August–28 September 1986.

24 *Heart in Exile: An Exhibition of Drawing, Painting, Sculpture and Photography by British-based Black Artists* ran from 4 September to 2 October 1983.

25 Members at the time (1982–9) were Menelik Shabazz, Milton Bryan, Imruh Bakari, Lazell Daley, Chuma Ukpadi, June Reid and Dada Imarogbe.

26 Scott MacKenzie (ed.), *Film Manifestos and Global Cinema Cultures: A Critical Anthology*, Oakland, CA, p.308. (This is also available online: https://www.jstor.org/table/10.2979/blackcamera. 6.2.58, accessed September 2021.)

27 Coco Fusco, *Young British and Black: The Work of Sankofa and Black Audio Film Collective*, New York 1988, p.25. (This is also available online: https://backend.ecstaticstatic.com/wp-content/uploads/2021/02/Young-British-Black.pdf.)

28 Keith Piper: https://keithpiper.info/gowestintro.html, accessed July 2021.

29 Mark Sealy, 'Portfolio: Rotimi Fani-Kayode – Desire in exile', *Tate Etc*, 26 October 2018: https://www.tate.org.uk/tate-etc/issue-44-autumn-2018/portfolio-rotimi-fani-kayode-desire-exile-mark-sealy, accessed July 2021.

30 Mark Sealy, *Decolonising the Camera: Photography in Racial Time*, Dagenham 2019, p.3.

31 After seeing Salt-N-Pepa play live in London, three friends formed She Rockers and gained the attention of rapper Chuck D, resulting in collaborations in the US.

32 Carl Stanley, 'Louder Than War Interview: DJ Normski. A photographic journey of hip-hop in the UK', 22 July 2013: https://louderthanwar.com/ltw-talk-to-normski-on-his-photographic-journey-of-uk-hip-hop/, accessed July 2021.

33 Ingrid Pollard: http://www.ingridpollard.com/oceans-apart---seleceted-images.html, accessed July 2021.

34 Shared in conversation with the author.

35 Ibid.

36 https://static1.squarespace.com/static/5797f07bf5e231d942a26c72/t/5ae9b0fa70a6ad102dbfc909/1525264636346/Donald+Rodney+-+Self+Portrait+Black+Men+Public+Enemy.pdf, accessed July 2021.

37 *Columbia Spectator*, vol. CXV, no.190, 5 December 1991: http://spectatorarchive.library.columbia.edu, accessed July 2021.

38 *Autograph Newsletter*, December 1991.

39 Clara Kim (ed.), *Steve McQueen*, exh. cat., London 2020, p.152.

40 Adrian Lobb, 'Sir Steve McQueen: "I was told a film with black leads wouldn't make money"', 28 February 2020: https://www.bigissue.com/latest/steve-mcqueen-i-was-told-a-movie-with-black-leads-wouldnt-make-any-money/, accessed July 2021.

41 'Ajamu challenges homophobia', *Trinidad & Tobago Guardian*, 24 July 2014: https://www.guardian.co.tt/article-6.2.385533.75cef56aad, accessed July 2021.

42 Jennie Baptiste in conversation with Christabel Johanson, Africanah.org: https://africanah.org/jennie-baptiste/, accessed July 2021.

43 Molara Wood, 'Emmanuel Jegede and the Fall of Time', 29 October 2005: http://molarawood.blogspot.com/2005/10/emmanuel-jegede-and-fall-of-time-by.html, accessed July 2021.

44 Carol Ann Dixon, 'Eugene Palmer: New Paintings', 15 March 2018: https://museumgeographies.com/2018/03/15/eugene-palmer-new-paintings/, accessed July 2021.

45 George 'Fowokan' Kelly: http://www.fowokan.com/words-and-vision/bronze/, accessed July 2021.

46 Turner Prize 1998: https://www.tate.org.uk/whats-on/tate-britain/exhibition/turner-prize-1998, accessed July 2021.

47 Charles Baudelaire's 'Fleurs du mal': https://fleursdumal.org/poem/119, accessed July 2021.

48 Sulter 1990, p.10.

49 Oliver Enwonwu, 'In conversation with Kimathi Donkor (part one)', 30 July 2019: https://www.omenkaonline.com/in-conversation-with-kimathi-donkor-part-one/, accessed July 2021.

50 Jackie Wullschläger, 'Hurvin Anderson: "I was the English boy in the Jamaican conversation"', *Financial Times*, 23 March 2021: https://www.ft.com/content/e70b781c-3144-43b9-9dcc-9197427899f4, accessed July 2021.

51 'A Q&A with… Hurvin Anderson, painter', 19 July 2016: https://www.a-n.co.uk/news/a-qa-with-hurvin-anderson-painter/, accessed July 2021.

52 'Lynette Yiadom-Boakye: Speaking through painting', *Tate Etc*, 13 October 2020: https://www.tate.org.uk/tate-etc/issue-50-autumn-2020/lynette-yiadom-boakye-antwaun-sargent-interview, accessed July 2021.

53 John Akomfrah on *The Unfinished Conversation*: https://vimeo.com/65409141, accessed July 2021.

54 Nosheen Iqbal, 'Anthea Hamilton on how she plans to top her Turner prize buttocks', 20 March 2018: https://www.theguardian.com/art and design/2018/mar/20/anthea-hamilton-turner-prize-buttocks-tate-britain-installation-duveen-commission, accessed July 2021.

55 Yinka Shonibare: https://www.youtube.com/watch?v=NJvv-HtRHQM, accessed July 2021.

56 Sokari Douglas Camp: https://sokari.co.uk/project/europe-supported-by-africa-and-america/, accessed July 2021.

57 Tim Adams, 'Hew Locke: "If I wasn't an artist, I'd be a historian"', *The Guardian*, 22 November 2015: https://www.theguardian.com/artanddesign/2015/nov/22/hew-locke-artist-interview-artist-and-empire-tate-britain, accessed July 2021.

58 'A Q&A with Helen Cammock', 2 November 2017: https://fisunguner.com/a-qa-with-helen-cammock/, accessed July 2021.

59 Barbara Walker: https://www.contemporaryartsociety.org/news/artist-to-watch/barbara-walker/, accessed July 2021.

60 Dave Lewis: https://grenadavenice.files.wordpress.com/2019/03/david-lewis.pdf, accessed July 2021.

61 Exhibition pamphlet for *Denzil Forrester: A Survey*, Stephen Friedman Gallery, 25 April–29 May 2019.

62 *Claudette Johnson: Pushing Back the Boundaries*, exh. cat., Rochdale Art Gallery, 13 October –17 November 1990: https://hollybush gardens.co.uk/wp/wp-content/uploads/Pushing-Back-the-Boundaries.pdf, accessed July 2021.

63 Rianna Jade Parker, 'How artist Phoebe Boswell teaches us to heal our wounds', *Frieze*, Issue 201, 4 February 2019: https://www.frieze.com/article/how-artist-phoebe-boswell-teaches-us-heal-our-wounds, accessed July 2021.

64 Walmsley 1992, p.318.

65 'Catch me if you can: An interview with Larry Achiampong', *The Quietus*, 3 November 2018: https://thequietus.com/articles/25609-larry-achiampong-interview, accessed July 2021.

66 'Interview with Alberta Whittle: "RESET"', 9–16 October 2020: http://thisistomorrow.info/articles/interview-with-alberta-whittle, accessed July 2021.

Suggested Reading

Nick Aikens and Elizabeth Robles, *The Place is Here: The Work of Black Artists in 1980s Britain*, Berlin 2019.

David. A. Bailey, Ian Baucom, Sonia Boyce and Leon Wainright, *Shades of Black: Assembling Black Arts in 1980s Britain*, Durham, NC 2005.

Eddie Chambers, *Black Artists in British Art: A History Since the 1950s*, New York 2014.

Eddie Chambers, *Roots & Culture: Cultural Politics in the Making of Black Britain*, London 2019.

Peter Fryer, *Staying Power: The History of Black People in Britain*, London 1984.

Coco Fusco, *Young British and Black: The Work of Sankofa and Black Audio Film Collective*, New York 1988. (This is also available online).

Paul Gilroy, *The Black Atlantic: Modernity and Double Consciousness*, New York 1993.

Paul Gilroy and Stuart Hall, *Black Britain: A Photographic History*, London 2011.

Ceri Hand, Chiedza Mhondoro and Zak Ové, *Get Up, Stand Up Now: Generations of Black Creative Pioneers*, exh. cat., London 2019.

Kobena Mercer, *Welcome to the Jungle: New Positions in Black Cultural Studies*, Abingdon-on-Thames 1994

Maud Sulter, *Passion: Discourses on Blackwomen's Creativity*, Chatham, Medway 1990.

Anne Walmsley, *The Caribbean Artists Movement 1966–1972: A Literary and Cultural History*, London 1992.

Credits

Every effort has been made to trace the copyright holders of the works illustrated and we apologise for any omissions or errors that may have been made.

PHOTOGRAPHY CREDITS

www.nickyakehurst.com p.49
Artimage 2021 pp.56–7, 60–1, 70–1, 75, 88–9
Artimage 2021. Courtesy the artist and Copperfield, London p.151
Courtesy the artist pp.63, 93, 99, 105, 113, 119, 141
Courtesy the artist and Autograph, London p.101
Courtesy the artist and Autograph, London. Photo: Zoe Maxwell pp.146–7
Courtesy the artist and Copperfield, London p.153
Courtesy the artist, Corvi-Mora, London, and Jack Shainman Gallery, New York p.123
Courtesy the artist and Cristea Roberts Gallery, London. Photo: Chris Keenan p.139
Courtesy the artist and Kate MacGarry, London p.137
Courtesy the artist and Stephen Friedman Gallery, London. Photo: Stephen White & Co p.142–3
Courtesy the artist, Thomas Dane Gallery and Marian Goodman Gallery p.103
Arts Council Collection, Southbank Centre, London p.97
Courtesy Autograph, London p.85
© Tim Bowditch front cover, p.45
Photo: Jonathan Greet. Courtesy the artist and October Gallery, London p.131
Photo: Damian Griffiths.

Courtesy the artist and Vigo Gallery, London p.135
Courtesy Isaac Julien p.79
Kirklees Collection: Huddersfield Art Gallery pp.2 (detail), 95
Leicester Museums & Galleries p.67
Colin Mills p.149
Museum of Youth Culture p.107
Normski Photography Archive p.87
Courtesy Horace Ové Archive p.39
Courtesy Keith Piper p.16
Rugby Art Gallery and Museum p.51
Courtesy Menelik Shabazz p.73
© Museums Sheffield/ Bridgeman Images pp.64–5
Courtesy Smoking Dogs Films and Lisson Gallery p.77
Courtesy Sotheby's p.35
© Tate pp.8, 13, 18, 22, 25, 26, 31, 36–7, 41, 43, 47, 55, 59, 69, 83, 115, 117, 121, 124–5, 127, 128–9, 133, 145
Courtesy Archives Van Abbemuseum, Eindhoven, the Netherlands. Photo: Nick Aikens p.81
© Victoria and Albert Museum, London p.91
Courtesy the Whitworth, The University of Manchester p.33
© Wolverhampton Art Gallery p.111

COPYRIGHT CREDITS

All works are © the artist unless otherwise stated below:

© Larry Achiampong. All Rights Reserved, DACS 2021 p.151
© John Akomfrah/ Smoking Dogs Films pp.124–5
© Raphael Albert, courtesy Autograph ABP p.43
Original print with kind permission of Big Broad and Massive; original poster

design by Wayne Fraser p.91
© Frank Bowling. All Rights Reserved, DACS 2021 pp.13, 35
© Sonia Boyce. All Rights Reserved, DACS 2021 p.75
© Vanley Burke. All Rights Reserved, DACS 2021 pp.56–7
© Pogus Caesar. All Rights Reserved, DACS 2021 pp.70–1
© Ceddo Film and Video Workshop p.73
© Estate of Uzo Egonu pp.36–7
© Armet Francis. All Rights Reserved, DACS 2021 pp.60–1
© Estate of Donald Locke p.41
© Hew Locke. All Rights Reserved, DACS 2021 p.133
© The McNish Trust/ Hull Traders Ltd. p.33
© Steve McQueen. Courtesy the artist, Thomas Dane Gallery and Marian Goodman Gallery p.103
© Estate of Ronald Moody p.31
© Dennis Morris – All Rights Reserved back cover, p.53
© Ingrid Pollard. All Rights Reserved, DACS 2021 pp.88–9
© Estate of Donald G. Rodney pp.18, 97
© Sankofa Film Collective p.79
© 2021 Estate of Khadija Saye, All Rights Reserved p.25
© Estate of Menelik Shabazz p.63
© Yinka Shonibare. Co-commissioned by HOUSE 2014 and Brighton Festival. Courtesy the artist and Stephen Friedman Gallery, London pp.128–9
© Smoking Dogs Films p.77
© Estate of Maud Sulter. All Rights Reserved, DACS 2021 p.117
© Estate of Aubrey Williams. All Rights Reserved, DACS 2021 p.55

Index

Page references in italics
indicate pages on which
artworks appear;
'exh.' = exhibition.